A Cowboy's Ride to Borderline

G. EdWARD ZINK

FOR CHRISTINE

There's calm in your eyes.

TABLE OF CONTENTS

Chapter 1

Although the necessary clues were made evident to him as early as the age of five, the implication of the little boy's October birthday was never obvious to his conscious thought processes until he was well into his 50s. Regardless of the timing of eventual revelation, memory of the circumstances of his conception and their sorry implication never dislodged from the sub rosa and transferred into the conscious awareness of the little boy. Whether or not he was genuinely loved *also* remained a concept yet to be fully developed.

As he grew older, the fact obscured he was an undesirable inconvenience from the outset served to confuse all subsequent expressions of parental love. Neither of his parents (much less the little boy) owned any understanding of the devastating influence this powerful dynamic would have on his future difficulty to function comfortably within his own skin.

As the layers of experience began to encompass his life, memories of an all too familiar terror fully embedded themselves into sinewy tendrils of scar tissue impinging upon receptors of what became abnormally operating brainwaves. Ultimately, the little boy in adulthood, would come to understand all too well that October the 1st is 273 days after New Year's Eve and he could no longer deny the suggestion that his very existence was the byproduct of nothing more significant than drunken lust run amok.

Although being a fetus within the womb of a good Catholic girl primarily saved him from abortion in 1954, restrictive

California law against that disgrace also played a part in sparing him a horrible alternative. Had things been otherwise, there's a good chance he may not have survived a scrape and hoovering.

It was not an easy road subsequently traveled; nevertheless, at road's end he would have few regrets. If indeed there was something, anything he could change throughout it all, he would find a way to erase from memory experiences of abject betrayal that destroyed his trust and compelled a lifelong fear of intimacy manifesting in the rejection of every significant relationship ever entering his world. Since the relativity of betrayal lies in the mind of the beholder, its natural connection to catharsis lies in the exposure of events unto the cleansing light of day. What follows is the unveiling of a twisted little boy's awful perception of disturbing experience.

* *

Shortly after turning age 5, he learned his daddy would have to spend time in the hospital to undergo an "operation"; the specifics of the procedure a mystery to him but the resolution Daddy sought was always made very plain. Daddy was unhappy that Mommy became pregnant with little sister "E.D.", a mere 13 months younger than he. The terms of the procedure remained a mystery until, as a young man fresh out of his junior high school birds and bees' class, he learned the procedure was called a vasectomy; yet the only thing the little boy knew at the time was that he would never, ever have either a little brother nor another little sister.

The young child of course, would comprehend none of the implications of this information; however, it was sufficient to cement the notion that the occasion of his sister's birth was an experience only distressing to his *daddy*. Mommy would remain in the little boy's mind completely guiltless of any culpability for the decision to forever prohibit him from getting the little brother he wanted.

About the time he turned age 9 it was clear to the little boy Daddy's "operation" was proof the birth of *any* other child beyond himself (in other words, sister E.D.) was in Daddy's world an undesirable happenstance; for which the possibility of recurrence now and forevermore surgically avoided. In spite of indicators pointing to another possible conclusion and the excuse given for the surgery in the first place, the little boy never held any suspicion *he* was ever considered by his mommy to have been anywhere near a mistake of nature. While on the other hand and deep within the little boy's subconscious, his daddy always remained to him very much suspect of harboring deep resentment toward the little boy's very existence. Curiously, Daddy never seemed to express to little sister E.D. the same measure of rage and bitterness he certainly held against the little boy.

Despite Daddy's subsequent violence against him, the fact that he was indeed a mistake of nature just like his little sister never actually occurred to him at any conscious level until many years morphed into faded memories. Even though his early childhood was rife with abuse, the little boy never once confronted the question whether his creation was an object of either parent's intention, much less he one among their most intimate desires.

Remaining clueless until pushing on his 54th year and only after tremendous introspection did he ever court doubt and finally compute the arithmetic of gestation, measuring the result against the dates on a calendar captured by a lifetime of painful experience. Mathematics verified what doubt always denied, binding his eventual surrender to cold reality by virtue of this one factor above all others. Only blunt soul-searching would ultimately disclose neither Mommy nor Daddy wanted *either* child when truth spilled its ugly guts.

The atrocities foist upon him began many years earlier on the first anniversary of his sister's birth, he a little tyke only two years old. By now, Daddy was well on his way to realizing that he erred when he married Mommy; in fact, the marriage had already briefly split and reconciled once prior to this particular celebratory occasion. Worse than bad decision making was the present trajectory of Daddy's career path – at 23 years of age, the word "loser" had gradually embossed itself across the rapid furrowing of his troubled brow. Underlying everything else, the little boy's daddy was himself bearing the burden of disguised and undefined child abuse hurled at him many years earlier by even his own mommy.

The young father was just a year out of service as an enlisted man in the United States Navy; recently exiled from the refuge he sought at seventeen to escape the mother he absolutely loathed and would later revile outright within ear-shot of his own two babies. For many of the early years of his young life, the vitriol his daddy spit Gramma's way **never** fell upon *her* ears; only the kids and their long-suffering mommy were forced to endure the obnoxious invectives directed at that old lady. Before the final chapter will herein be written, Daddy will actually prove more coward than loser.

Sister E.D.'s 1st birthday would come along soon after "Grampa" had thrown his floundering son a lifeline, securing for him a job as a route salesman driving a bread truck. The job, offered to him by the bakery where "Grampa" was a very high-level sales executive, required the little boy's daddy to deliver Weber's bread, Roman Meal products, and Dolly Madison cakes to various supermarkets along his own sales route in select Orange County neighborhoods. Despite "Grampa's" influence affecting his hiring, the little boy's daddy resented the gesture, which reflexively operated to elevate the heat under a simmering former Navy frogman specializing just three years earlier implementing high-explosives against military targets in foreign lands. The circumstances of undesirable reliance upon the largesse of his own "daddy" generated in the man a personal resentment with no other outlet in which to boil-over except the very hearth and home he so carelessly and hastily sired.

With Daddy's (but not Mommy's) parents present on this day of celebration, the entire group would watch in amazement as the

25-month-old boy provoked his daddy into viciously attacking him in retaliation for a heinous effrontery. Although it was the first such incident where the adult spun totally out of control at the little boy's inadvertent instigation, it was far from the last attack of its kind.

Along with a career in the Navy as an underwater demolitions man and before the sailor was himself a daddy; he also moonlighted (after a fashion) as a would-be underground boxer, very much in the vein of Clint Eastwood's character Philo Beddoe in the movie "Any Which Way But Loose". Apparently, Daddy wasn't very good at this avocation and regularly had the snot beaten out of him. His face took so much abuse in his failed pugilistic endeavors that his nose was literally spread 1/3rd the way across his face and protruded nearly 2 inches out into public airspace. The man's nose was beyond enormous and, as it turned out on that particular day, it also proved to be an inviting object of the little boy's immediate teething needs.

It was on the occasion that a lit candle on birthday cake was offered sister E.D., as Daddy held the little boy to his chest, that the impetuous toddler lifted up his little head and bit his daddy squarely on the nose…you know, a little "love bite". Unfortunately, Daddy's response was far from loving and quite instantaneous, intending to teach the little boy a lesson he shouldn't soon forget and would be among the earliest living memories the little boy would take with him into adulthood. Payback would be the favor brutally returned upon the child's forearm, which Daddy bit so hard that a blood-red hematoma would swell that area the size of a Ping-Pong ball; the mark lasted weeks before finally vanishing away through the inevitable sloughing of human growth.

Such behavior was the typical manner in which the little boy would later learn of all his daddy's displeasure, immediately and well into the future. These unfortunate lessons of obedience were so often administered just to him and never unto sister E.D., the confused little boy's entire frame of reference became so distorted he began to believe *he* was the sole source of every worldly thing his daddy hated. Regrettably, these unfortunate "lessons" were infused so early of age in the child they became forever etched in the little boy's psyche and remained essentially unabated for a lifetime.

Hovering somewhere in the haze of memory between this first assault and the next most memorable instance of disloyalty occurred as he was nearing his fourth birthday; the occasion of a tonsillectomy would spawn his lifelong distrust of medicine in general and doctors in particular. The extent of the memory a hideous nightmare of utter helplessness - a little boy left all alone - prone under huge parabolic lamps and in the care of space aliens swathed head-to-toe in green scrubs.

As his expanding awareness of things external to him greeted new knowledge and though not yet fully understanding why, he soon discovered through the haze of medical upheaval the marital family had acrimoniously split itself asunder. Even worse was notification that once his stay in the hospital terminated, he would thenceforth be living with Mommy's parents and their other two children and would no longer be living at all with his daddy.

Sure, sister E.D. and his mommy would be living under the same new roof as he; nevertheless, a major disruption would ensue and upset the lives of all concerned. Everyone that is, except his daddy, who would otherwise remain unfazed by the turmoil of separation and relocation. Indeed, under the refreshing aura of a splintered family, Daddy would even hook-up with a little co-ed and future home wrecker with giant tits. Although it will later prove true, this woman's active contribution to the terror of emotional abuse underlying the family dynamic was at this point in the chronology of events an unknown entity. Eventually, the level of this woman's investment in their daddy will be revealed for all its callous selfishness.

Their new home would be under the roof provided by Grampa Freddie, a "milkman" by trade who drove a delivery truck for Altadena Dairy; a job for which he left home at 3 A.M. six days a week and Gramma Frances, who worked 6 hours a day in a dress shop, while still caring for her own two homebound teenagers. As his fourth year commenced, the little boy would develop a bond with his Uncle Frankie, an ambitious young man at seventeen with his own job, car, and a girlfriend, too. In contrast, the little boy didn't much care for Mommy's parents or her little sister Aunt Carolyn since he found them a little creepy and not nearly as generous and fun to be around as were his daddy's parents, whom he felt treated him much more affectionately.

Irrespective of his disconnect with the others, he adored his Uncle Frankie and would substitute the relationship for that of his missing father; luckily for the little boy, Frankie always graciously accepted the inclusion of his company. Tagging along on many of the mindless excursions typical of a teenager, doing so wherever Frankie's Dodge Dart happened to meander in and around the city of Pasadena, the little boy developed quite a fondness for the simple pleasure of just motoring about. Most memorably, such excursions brought them on more than one occasion to Mount Wilson's Chancery Flats campground, where they (sometimes also with Frankie's high school sweetheart, Pam) would hike the trails and generally, just fool around in the woods.

These day trips would always find the little boy gasping for breath through lungs aching from thin mountain air, coupled with thick brown smog rising upslope from the very much-polluted Los Angeles basin below. Afterward, they would sometimes stop for lunch at the In-n-Out Burger drive-thru in Arcadia. His time spent with Uncle Frankie would be among the last of the really good times and themselves very short-lived, as Frankie would soon leave the nest by joining the United States Air Force. Sad was the little boy on the day of Frankie's departure to South Korea where he would perform his patriotic duty in America's service as a disc jockey for the Airbases' on-post radio station.

Even if it were there for others to appreciate, he never found any underlying charm about the ancient house on Oneida Street in

Pasadena; from day one everything about the place was always very spooky to the little boy. Constructed in 1909, the house was relatively small at 1,100 square feet, with only three bedrooms plus a sunroom where the child vagabonds were to be encamped. Mommy and sister "Caro" shared a bedroom; Uncle Frankie had his own room while the little boy and sister E.D. bunked in the sunroom, the only access to which was through Gramma 'n Grampa's bedroom. The land upon which the house stood was quite large with acreage enough for one other house as well; a larger house that stood at the head of the curved driveway on the other side of, and quite obscured by, a very tall hedgerow. This other residence faced the street while the little boy's new house faced the hedges obscuring the other folk's backyard.

There were two memorable attributes to the house's construction; one feature contributing to the creepiness of the place was a large dusty and junk cluttered basement. The other feature of this house, one which would soon hold terrible significance to the little boy, was the presence of a throwback to a bygone era; a glass-paned door that separated the living room from his grandparent's bedroom and the interconnected sunroom. As events would unfold, the adverse consequences became mostly attributable to a thick, olive-green velvet drapery hanging on the bedroom side of the door; a horrible shroud entirely covering the 18 glass panes divided by wooden muntins embedded into the door's framework. The drapery's purpose was, of course, to secure the privacy of the Gram's master bedroom.

In the summer of his fourth year, the little boy's mommy took a job as a typist. Because Gramma 'n Grampa each worked steady jobs, he and sister E.D. were under the care of their two teenage children during the daytime; either Uncle Frankie or Aunt Caro, she only fifteen years of age at the time. In spite of their familial dislocation, the peculiar new home and the old fogey grandparents, this was perhaps the most carefree summer the little boy would ever enjoy; even unto transition into his own fogey-hood.

As the days that summer grew shorter, a new turmoil would

engulf the little boy in a large way. First, his new surrogate daddy, Uncle Frankie left home for the Air Force and South Korea. Then, and quite by surprise, he would learn that Aunt Caro would rejoin her junior year high school class and since the Grams each had jobs occupying their daytime, the nomadic children would be commencing schooling much sooner than the little boy had been expecting.

When his mommy informed him of this new reality, he did not greet the news with open arms and a whoop and a holler and indeed became very, very distressed. As the day of reckoning arrived, sister E.D. simply and courageously took the entry into "nursery school" (daycare) absolutely nonplused; on the other hand, the little boy made such a scene it belied the maturity level of his four years. Suffice to say, he played the little drama prince boy-brat that morning to award winning, yet no availing effect.

Of course, once the fear of the unknown wore off, all was well and the children settled down into a 4 or 5-hour routine away from home and under the guardianship of professional childcare. Afterward, they would return to the creepy old house and usually remained under the care of Aunt Caro until Mommy returned home from her typist job. For the little boy, these new schooldays wouldn't last a fortnight before coming to a terrible end that would be the first, but not the last, bullet he would dodge serendipitously resulting in death cheated. Fortunately for him, and in the nick of sweet Jesus, an angel presented itself that day, personified in the pimply-faced Aunt Caro.

All during the family's exile to Pasadena, Daddy exhibited absolutely no interest in maintaining any contact with them whatsoever. As the passage of time offered its hindsight, Daddy could be found busy courting the woman who, in 6 short years, would become his future ex-wife. Indeed, under other more fortuitous circumstances she may well have hastened her eventual wedding date; unfortunately, the little boy's brush with death would indefinitely put Daddy's burgeoning new relationship on the back burner. Ultimately, ambition got the best of him and he would be forced by tragedy to return to his family in order to achieve a new career goal.

All during the dissolution of the family unit, the little boy's daddy, driving the bread truck by day, was also taking classes (where he met his new girlfriend, a co-ed working as the teacher's assistant) and seeking a high school diploma by night. Daddy's educational motivation was the first component of a plan to modify his career path by way of a detour through the Los Angeles Police Academy.

On a fateful day that September at mid-afternoon and not yet accepted into the police academy, when crisis consumed the family unit, Daddy's only course of action would be to return to the nest or risk wholesale rejection by the Los Angeles Police Department and dashing his opportunity to be an L.A. cop. After all, how would he ever justify (during his pre-academy interview) leaving his wife and two children behind for some bimbo, while his little son was in the hospital fighting for his life? No, if he wanted to be a Los Angeles police officer *now*…he would have to make his existing family whole again…and pray the little boy didn't die before reconciliation.

Had he died from his injury, aside from the gargantuan loss of blood, the cause would have been directly attributable to a lack of proper adult supervision, the absence of which Daddy would have trouble living down. In 1959, the hiring standards of the L.A.P.D. were very strict with considerable weight given to men with high moral character and the horrible incident would be impossible to hide from official scrutiny. Therefore, Daddy's plan to abandon his family, given the incident, would not bode well for successful admittance into one of America's most staid and venerated police academies.

Although adult supervision was nowhere onsite, there was indeed present that day a guardian angel that enveloped the little boy in its embrace and not for the last time in his life, either.

No one can possibly know who actually instigated the activity, but the game hide-and-go-seek would briefly occupy sister E.D. and the little boy one day after the children returned from daycare. Unfortunately, the harrowing accident would not allow even one round of the game, which ended with the little boy screaming in aguish and adrenaline-laced fear amid a tremendous amount of bloodshed…his own. While Aunt Caro was counting up to 100, the children were individually casting about looking for a satisfactory place to hide. Of course, this game they were playing within the confines of the ancient house, at once bereft of decrepit floor covering and recently adorned with expensive and spanking new Berber-style carpeting.

What happened next seemed to play itself out in slow-motion; yet, the little boy's reactions were conducted at full gallop and motivated entirely by utter panic in which he was certain he was going to lose his life. The immediate sensation he felt, beyond the instantaneously abject fear that oddly tended to overwhelm the physical pain, was a rather strange sense of helplessness that his personal boundaries had been heinously violated. The gaping opening in his flesh and muscle unmistakable evidence he was now powerless to prevent his life from simply oozing through a severed brachial artery and into the new carpeting. Indeed, his greatest measure of true discomfort only visited him about 10 days later when the 80 or so stitches were removed from the skin of his inner bicep; during a procedure in which he wailed from physical agony a hundred times more intense than the actual shredding of the arm itself.

He owes his life saved that day to his Aunt Caro, for without her presence of mind to corral the panicking boy, stanch the bleeding with bath towels and call the authorities, he surely would have bled to death. From the instant Aunt Caro took charge and in spite of his youth, he was always keenly aware of the bullet he dodged and the gratitude he owed his auntie for her calm bravery and the stoic valor she demonstrated that day.

Sadly, and wrongly or otherwise, the little boy would for

years hold the blame for the incident over little sister E.D.'s head. His every recollection of events would forever hold that the glass in the door *only* broke as he (following her into the master bedroom from the living room) pushed on the glass-paned door, at once ajar, at the same moment his sister was obsessed in the act of latching it closed. Even though well aware of the heavy drapery covering the glass panes and obscuring both children's vision, the way he saw it there was no logical reason for that door not to open for him except for her effort alone denying him the desired entry.

What is certain… a glass pane broke, his little arm filleted; whether or not sister E.D. was *aware* at the time the little boy wished access to the hiding spot she defended would forevermore be in doubt. For her part, his sister would never acknowledge that she even touched the door; much less ever admitting she was trying to close it at that particular moment. Of course, as years advanced, the little boy would come to recognize the foolishness of time wasted trying to rationalize the irrationality of a 4-year-old boy's expectation of a 3-year-old girl's spatial awareness.

The Pasadena city police arrived at that funky old blood-soaked house before the ambulance did and the officers made the snap decision to transport him immediately to the hospital rather than wait for the medics. As the policeman clutched the wounded little boy to his chest and carried him from the house to the patrol car, a vision revealed that would forever remain his earliest, most vivid childhood memory carried with him into manhood. At the exact moment they exited the house, the little boy's mother walked around the bend in the hedgerow obscuring the house on the south side of that long driveway, having just moments earlier been dropped off at the curb by her carpool and ending her workday, only to view her bloodied son in dire straits, clutched in the arms of a uniformed policeman.

While Aunt Caro stayed behind to look after sister E.D., the little boy and his mommy took refuge in the back seat of a police car that would soon be speeding down Pasadena's sleepy residential streets while the siren was screaming at everyone within earshot that a little boy was in trouble and they had better get the hell out of the way. He was traveling faster, faster than ever before but since he couldn't see out of the car's windows, he had no opportunity to experience any further excitement that day and slipped into an unconsciousness unsettling to his mommy.

Prior to the occasion of the frightful suture removal, the only other event of significance occurring at the hospital, which melded into the little boy's memory, would be the bedside reunion with his daddy for the first time since relocating to Pasadena months earlier. Though the visit was brief and the little boy somewhat delirious, it was immediately obvious to him this near-death incident was catalyst for a permanent reconciliation and the new beginning for a fractured family. He was assured by his daddy when he returned home it would be to a new house just for the four of them and Mommy's relatives would be spared further abuse from their eldest daughter's own growing problem children.

Chapter 2

*D*uring the next three days, blood from strangers oozed into his veins through tubing that left behind a permanent scar on the instep side of his right ankle. When finally discharged after twelve days recuperation, he left the hospital with significant nerve damage and a slight deformity to his right hand due to ancillary tendon and muscle damage deep within the gaping, hook-shaped wound.

The anticipated reunion with his newly reconciled parents really did nothing to buoy his spirits since the little boy would have to resume some kind of civil relationship with the death-dealing three-year-old sister, E.D. Although he would grant her a somewhat forced absolution, the sibling's relationship would for a while contain a certain resentment-based contentiousness; neither child guiltless in the sense each harbored bad memories about the incident and its occurrence.

The young family, once again comprising all members, would reunite at their new apartment about 4 or 5 blocks down the road from Gramma 'n Grampa's house with the newly savaged carpeting. Little more than 600 sq. ft., the flat was an addition built above a converted two-car garage originally intended for the main residence – a duplex - constructed in the 1920s. Below their apartment, one half of the garage was isolated as a private storage area and the other half constructed as a tiny apartment occupied by the family's occasional babysitter, the crotchety, white-haired septuagenarian widow, Mrs. Ness.

All during these early years the little boy was raised under the "spare the rod" theory of child rearing; the so-called "time-out" a vision of utopia reserved for future progressive wack-jobs. Even so, during his first 6 or 7 years, he never demonstrated a behavior that ever caused his mommy to administer anything worse than physically grabbing between her thumb and forefinger either ear and twisting it severely to impress upon him her standards of proper citizenship.

Ironically, and aside from the nose/arm-biting tit-for-tat of years earlier, any occasional daddy administered corporal punishment had not as yet impacted any impressionable memory. Unfortunately, here at the Virginia Avenue apartment, not only would Daddy begin to assault him physically, the little boy would seemingly find personal betrayal at almost every crossroads being dispatched by family and friends alike.

Life after his fifth birthday was relatively calm and uneventful and while sister E.D. stayed home under the care of the ever-so-creepy Mrs. Ness, the little boy would go to kindergarten at Hamilton Elementary School. He would walk to and from the Virginia Avenue apartment with his new best friend, a kid his age named Bradley who lived four doors just up the street.

The only outliers from the usual daily routine were Daddy's aforementioned vasectomy; and shortly thereafter, Mommy became bedridden for about ten days with a bout of pleurisy that required treatment with applications of disgusting "mustard plasters" on her back. As for the little boy, his only lasting memory resulted from another laceration to one of his hands, deep enough to require stitches, which occurred one evening after supper and requiring a trip to the emergency room. On this particular occasion the little boy injured himself while testing the limitations in the strength of a water glass when a person tries to shove inside too many ice cubes.

His fifth year of age (being a sort of grace period granted almost as consolation for the trauma he had endured the year prior) eventually transitioned into his sixth and almost as if a switch was thrown, for the next three and a half years the only certainty the little boy would know would be fear and insecurity. Any moments of reprieve from the state of unpredictability of outcomes were few and tempered with pervasive feelings of dread that any simple thing would set his daddy's internal rage into unbridled overdrive.

Was it a coincidence this behavior would manifest about the same time Daddy began his policeman's career as a cadet in training? That assessment is left to the reader whom must first be advised that never did his daddy's new career focus seem motivated by the desire to *help* anyone; this particular Los Angeles policeman was only motivated by the possibility that he was gonna get to crack open some perp's head someday with a Maplewood baton. Nevertheless, a change would soon be taking place in the life of his son; while Daddy, now given a policeman's authority, would be responsible for the bulk of disruption to a little boy's sense of security and the resulting human misery.

Things began to sour in the relationship between the little boy and his daddy one afternoon of the dog days during his summer vacation from school between kindergarten and 1st grade.

It was bad enough that the first horrible incident was a personal attack, even eye-witnessed by the other neighborhood children, including Bradley and his little sister. Worse still and subsequent to the first horrible incident, other events stemming from Bradley's general direction would eventually culminate in the little boy and sister E.D. having contact with Bradley and family severely restricted. The little boy would be forced by circumstance to abandon in distrust his best and only friend; while the icing on the cake came after the little boy suffered a beating from Daddy so severe, he was convinced should never have happened but for his acquaintance with the other boy in the first place.

His pal Bradley was the older of two children and he too had a little sister E.D.'s age, so the children all played together after school and on weekends. These kids were from a presumably well-adjusted family of four who lived in a 3 bedroom house featuring, much like the lot on which the little boy lived, a detached garage that also housed a tenant unrelated to the residents of the house. Soon after moving into their new apartment, the tenant living in the garage at Bradley's place was deemed by the little boy's parents to be a drunkard and was to be avoided at all times, by both the little boy and sister E.D.

The four children would alternately all play together or either the two boys would go about doing things separate from the two girls, and vice versa. Sometimes one or two other children living nearby would play with these kids, as well. All these activities either occurred after school, on weekends and vacation days, either up at Bradley's house or in a little courtyard that was located in the space between the garage and the duplex on the property, where the little boy's apartment overlooked the whole area.

The home immediately to the north was another duplex and this residence also shared the courtyard area adjoining the family's apartment. The tenant to the rear unit of the duplex was a twenty-something man named Conrad who rode a motorcycle that, to all the kids, seemed like the devil's machine straight out of Brando's The Wild One. It could have been a Vespa scooter or even a Harley for all they knew; but that didn't matter, Conrad was a badass and all the kids, especially the little boy, idolized the image of what might be described a rebellious nature. He was a pretty good kid, even a responsible young man, but the presence of the motorcycle was all that the little boy needed to properly categorize what kind of man that was this Conrad fellow. Essentially, the little boy had a thing for motorcycles and Conrad received his adulation for his obvious ability to manhandle the mechanical beast adorned black on chrome.

While the children were this day ostensibly under the care of the aged Mrs. Ness and Mommy was at work, Daddy soon would be home from a day at police academy to relieve the old fossil from her babysitting chores. With no indication of the babysitter's whereabouts, all and sundry of the children of the little boy's family, Bradley and his sister, plus one or two other neighbor kids were all in the courtyard "interacting" with good friend and noted biker Conrad; he being in the process of polishing up the demon ride. Basically, the kids were all teasing him for and with a behavior of no memorable significance. Whatever was said at the time is irrelevant; suffice in the knowledge that all the kids participated and all of it was just good-natured fun with no hint of vitriol whatsoever. Moreover, even though he was the brunt of it, good-old patient Conrad was totally cool with all the taunting and childish banter.

There's no way to know exactly what he said at the time, but there is no doubt that the words spoken to Conrad were coming through the little boy's lips. Additionally, there's no way to know just why what was said caused his daddy to go so instantly ballistic and transmit himself to planet Berzerko, but that is precisely where one of Los Angeles' future "finest" went the moment he first entered the courtyard and observed the amiable rumpus.

Daddy's retribution, focused entirely upon the little boy, was swiftly executed right under the disbelieving eyes of rest of his little chums, including the not entirely guiltless sister E.D. Yes, the little angel herself was right alongside gently taunting Conrad the biker with all the rest of the little brats. Indeed, that Daddy pin-pointed all his attention upon his son was true, however the ogre did insist that the other children involved should ideally receive a demonstration of what he would do to them, had they too happened to reside in that cramped apartment overlooking the tumult below.

Although the complete picture of the family dynamic has thus far been somewhat glossed over, the fact is by this point in time the little boy was no stranger to corporal punishment meted out by his daddy. Until this moment all such punishment he ever administered to son was typically a "spanking"; usually five or so swats with bare hand upon the little boy's butt. However, on this particular occasion, his daddy became so infuriated that he grabbed the little boy and stripped off his trousers *and* underpants; then, the man sat down on a short concrete block wall that served to divide the courtyard from the barbecue area of the yard where he bare-hand spanked his little boy's bare little ass for what seemed to the younger an eternity.

There were a range of emotions that entered his consciousness all at once competing for recognition of, and demand for the status of supremacy over the others; his mind grasping for something, anything, to attach the chaos of absurd circumstances to some measure of experiential reality. Above it all, he was at first beset by complete disbelief coupled with an irresistible sense of confusion neither of which helped him resolve a calculus so abrupt and incomprehensible. As the incident unfolded and he found himself helplessly the star of some sick psychodrama orchestrated by a frenzied madman, fear and embarrassment supplanted his earlier shock and incredulity.

With nothing in his prior experience from which to grasp for reassurance, panic became the little boy's overarching motivational factor and when that too offered no route to salvation, the only avenue left him was to suffer through a demonstration of the most awful kind of humiliation while his entire posse watched it all unfold in real time. The embarrassment of being punished in the presence of his friends was one thing; that he was stripped naked having his bare ass paddled in the presence of the other children was another kind of shame. Worse still for him was the much more ignominious fact that everybody in the world now knew this little boy was, not only the offspring of a knuckle-dragging brute, but *obviously* cut from the same bolt of cloth.

When it was all over and the other children sent home, the little boy thereafter received the standard follow-up punishment that always came with the humiliation of which his daddy himself now suffered. Obviously culpable, Daddy would assure the little boy that the punishment handed down hurt Daddy much more than it hurt the child and then he'd resort to guilt-tripping the child for causing an adult to act as he just did.

As if disgrace overwhelmed his emotions and he could no longer stand the sight of the object of his rage, the little boy was banished to his bedroom and expected to retire and go to sleep and do it without supper, too. This pattern would repeat as his daddy and occasionally Mommy, too, could never muster courage to face the child after administering their special brand of discipline. In effort to cleanse himself of his own guilt, Daddy would initiate the first of many similar applications to come and the little boy was exiled to his room for the rest of that day/evening; however, not before being informed that the punishment inflicted on the little boy was indeed not nearly as severe as the pain in Daddy's heart for having to be the administrator.

One day while walking home from 1st grade at Hamilton, Bradley taught the little boy a skill he would seize upon for the rest of his lifetime; although he was compelled to disguise all manifestations of the talent from his parents for the next 20 years or so. It seems Bradley was of the belief that people and things that displeased him were well deserving of the immediate vocal retort, "fuck you" to all and sundry that crossed his path. On this particular day the little boy, being quite an apt pupil and a real natural, would yell, "fuck you" along with Bradley at every passerby whether standing on human feet or confined within some vehicle. Discretion mattered little as social convention was abandoned by two little 6-year-old hellions let loose on the streets of Pasadena. "Fuck you!" "And…fuck you, too!" "Hey mister, fuck you!"

Such was the level of skill so proudly held this afternoon that, while Daddy was at police academy and Mommy was feeding her babies early supper, little sister E.D. preposterously offered the little boy an opinion about something at variance with his belief eliciting an immediate "fuck you, E.D.", which he blithely hurled her way. Unfortunately for him, those sound waves were not confined to sister E.D.'s ears only; nay, Mommy too caught wind of the outburst and took instant exception, with which she coupled backhanded action to the side of his peevish little face. Strangely, even though the extent of Daddy's brutality would not yet manifest, he was instantly paralyzed by the thought Mommy would tell Daddy of this particular blunder. Given Daddy's reaction to the

Conrad incident, all the little boy could be sure of was this… God forbid Daddy find out anything about this, lest his ass soon be dad-grassified.

For whatever reason, Mommy never told his daddy about the matter and there's no telling the reason why she didn't. Perhaps it was because he immediately ratted out Bradley as the instigator and Mommy already branded as suspect the other boy's basic civility. After all, what kind of people would allow a slovenly drunkard so near their own children by granting him permanent tenancy in their garage? Now this punk was teaching her little boy speech decidedly unacceptable for a child baptized in the Roman Catholic faith. . Although his mommy did immediately militate against the little boy's further expressions of impudent obscenity, nevertheless trouble began to brew.

Possibly because of an inter-parental complaint from his mommy to Bradley's parents over the "fuck you" incident, or maybe it stemmed from the observable weaknesses within the family unit revealed during the Conrad incident; nevertheless, a few weeks later the little boy was aroused from his sleep and forced to answer an inquiry of the Pasadena police department, in what seemed to him were the wee hours of morning. Being a six-year-old and being given the "third degree" was bad enough, but what made it all the more so was that his own daddy seemed to gleefully join the Pasadena cops in making the false accusations; while the old bastard did nothing to defend his son's innocence, he otherwise planted a bulb of ever-flowering distrust that never withered even after the season of their relationship long since had passed.

The circumstance bringing the cops to their home that night was the revelation that Bradley was implicated in a car tire-slashing incident and falsely fingered the little boy as either his accomplice or the real guilty party sans Bradley; such nuanced distinction was forever a mystery to the accused. Regrettably, a false indictment originating with his best friend was the reason for the unwelcome late-night interruption. What otherwise should have been dreams of innocence, became a living and lifelong nightmare as the little boy's ability to trust people in general and authority in particular began unraveling that very night. Moreover, the entire experience cemented only one idea of concrete significance; the little boy could never count on his daddy "to have his back" under any circumstances in the future.

As it turned out the coppers would have nothing on him; and, even though guilt was adamantly denied and some measure of suspicion would linger temporarily over the little boy, his parents no longer held valid the expectation that Bradley had a positive influence upon the little boy. However, they were practical enough to realize they couldn't just forbid the little boy all contact with his best friend and literal classmate. Although the excuse was that Mommy and Daddy feared their kids were not staying far enough away from the drunken tenant of Bradley's garage, the parent's real motivation was more complex than that which was expressed.

For the immediate future the new family rule was simple, the little boy and sister E.D. were forbidden to go to Bradley's house, just four doors up the street. Period. Bradley and the little boy could still walk to school together and the kids could all still play together; however, they could go nowhere near Bradley's house evermore.

With the little boy's and his sister's personalities having thus far developed, evident were two distinct behaviors each child possessed. The little boy was able to discern parental intent and act accordingly. Alternatively, by the age of 5, the heretofore Teflon-coated sister E.D. always found a way to interpret her parent's wishes by analyzing what was left out of a discussion and inevitably finding a way to seize upon any evidence supporting the conclusion an exemption was most certainly carved out especially for her.

Such was the nature of the next horrifying event. It was summertime; the little boy made it through 1st grade and his sister, kindergarten. It would be their last summer residing in Pasadena and their daddy would soon graduate as a bona fide Los Angeles police officer. The means whereby sister E.D. acquired the postcard addressed to Bradley's family would remain unanswered; once events unfolded there was no time to analyze causation anyway. Afterward, well, the little boy was just glad to have survived the attack with nothing more than a few bruises and a young body chock full of nature's own pick-me-up...pure adrenaline speedily coursing through his veins.

The only thing the little boy knew beforehand was that his mommy handed him the errant mailer and requested he go up the street real quick and return it *for her*; so Mommy didn't have to take it herself to the otherwise off-limits Bradley's house. Except, while the little boy was definitely forbidden to visit that place, Mommy wasn't. However, being Mommy's good little man, what else was there for him to do but to comply with her wish? After all, he would get see his friend for a few minutes and perhaps this errand would help break the ice for the parents to revisit their decision to isolate the children from each other.

They say timing is everything. Although the 6-year-old boy was unaware people said such things, on this day the timing of Mommy's demand for the return of the postcard very much coincided with the convergence of the little boy's exit from Bradley's front door at the exact moment his daddy would be driving down Virginia Avenue concluding a day at the police academy. As their eyes met while crossing paths, one pair turned a blood red and the other pair instantly began to seek a niche of refuge. All at once his daddy stopped his car, leapt out the driver's door and all too quickly grabbed the little boy with little feet dangling off the asphalt, left helplessly pondering a direction in which to flee but no ground underneath upon which to gain any traction.

In the meantime, his mommy was dispatching the impish sister E.D. to her bedroom for the rest of the day...she to get in bed, forget all about her supper, and lay low as possible until the morrow. Mommy did not yet know the shit was about to fly inside that little apartment in the manner that it would; however, as the day was getting late and E.D. did indeed deserve some form of correction, such would be best if Mommy took care of the matter before Daddy got home and she knew that fact well and good. What she didn't realize by then was that time had been cut too close and she had inadvertently sent her little boy barefoot into a snake pit.

Even though Mommy was doing what she could to minimize any collateral damage concerning E.D.'s fate, she had no idea that Daddy had already caught the little boy totally red-handed. After all the dust settled and the little boy learned of the leniency of sister E.D.'s punishment compared to the brutality he suffered for the crime *she* committed; dismay would be a most generous understatement of his immediate emotion. To the little boy, it was just another example how his precocious and slippery little sister skated away once again, never herself falling through the thin ice of existence in this dementedly dysfunctional household.

When they returned in Daddy's car to the apartment, Daddy dragged him by his left arm from the car, across the driveway and up the stairs; all the while the little boy was sort of two stepping on his tippy-toes in effort to keep up and not having his shoulder dislocated in the process. They entered the apartment together a whirlwind, for Mommy had no inkling of what would greet her when the front door flew open. Before she could say anything, Daddy continued dragging his son into Mommy and Daddy's bedroom, where he shut and locked the door behind them.

After the door was closed and locked and the little boy helplessly awaited his fate, his daddy rummaged around the shelf in the closet hidden behind two flimsy sliding doors while excitedly looking for something in particular. This event of disobedience turned into an occasion in which Daddy was finally able to put to good use one of the new pieces of equipment he had to purchase as part of his policeman's uniform. No...and thankfully he did not yet possess any firearms. However, he did just days earlier purchase a latigo leather belt known as a Sam

Browne. A standard policeman's belt ¼" thick, 2" wide, made to fit a 36-inch waste and brand new, with the basket weave pattern embossed throughout and polished a shiny black. Fortunately, it was only the belt with none of the other accoutrements that would otherwise attach to an actual cop's service belt.

Despite what the liberal social engineering pussies try to claim, there is an upside to child abuse; sadly, the benefit is somewhat rooted in Darwinism, another liberal canard. Well, fuck the pointy-heads, there *is* a socially redeeming aspect to be found here and this is it… In the experience of this particular little boy, his pain threshold became quite elevated with the passing of every subsequent session with his high-strung and short-tempered daddy. Essentially, nature allowed him to learn how to take a punch.

Gradually, the little boy would retreat internally by simply bathing in the numbness sweeping over and further desensitizing him with every subsequent abusive episode; the accumulation of blows making numb the id and perpetuating an insensitivity over time easier to find and upon which to comfortably rely as a natural self-defense mechanism. Comfortably, numb…as the song goes.

Receding inward, the beating this time seemed strangely over with before it even started. Certainly, the little boy was indeed whipped that afternoon with that never before worn L.A.P.D. approved duty belt. Various neurotransmitters, massive quantities of adrenaline, serotonin, and dopamine surging within, his thoughts of flight overwhelming any inquiry why his daddy chose this particular implement to express his monumental displeasure. More likely than not, the instrument was a harkening back to the very treatment he suffered from his own mother; who regularly beat her son with her own leather strap. Of course, it would be several more years before the little boy ever gleaned inkling that Gramma Beryl was herself the primary source of his daddy's own personal dementia.

His daddy's deep-seated frustration at once satisfied via the unbridled flailing upon the back of his young son, the little boy held little doubt that his next stop would be straight to bedtime without supper; even though it was barely 5 o'clock. And since things spun out of control so rapidly, Daddy was very much unaware of sister E.D.'s guilt and that she too was concurrently enduring corrective measures for her part in this whole sordid mess.

Therefore, when the locked door opened and his daddy attempted to expel the little boy to the bedroom the two children shared, his mommy was forced to step in and lay out an explanation of the actual events that transpired before he steered his car onto their street that afternoon. To her credit, when his mommy could actually manage the opportunity to get a word in edgewise without getting her own head blown off, she did so forcefully enough to see to it that her son would be exonerated in the eyes of his very scary daddy.

Did he receive consolation or vindication? Maybe a little of each; sister E.D. herself was for once suffering for her sins and was locked down tight for the night, while the little boy was treated to a rare game of catch with his daddy out on the driveway, where they played till way past dark.

"You know son, that hurt me a lot more than it hurt you."

"I'm sorry, Daddy. I'll try to do better next time."

Chapter 3

*T'*he relocation from Pasadena was motivated by his daddy's induction into the Los Angeles Police Department and both children would begin the new school year at Tarzana Elementary School. Located in a tranquil suburb of the southwest portion of the San Fernando Valley and situated just north, northwest of the heart of Los Angeles, the family moved into a well-worn three-bedroom rental house on Collins Street. Their house was one door away from the intersection at Wilbur Avenue; the other side of which his new school was located and was a street deemed so hazardous to the school children that a crossing guard was required during school hours. Wilbur Avenue extended north to south through the length of the belly of the Valley.

It was September of 1961; little sister E.D. began her 1st grade of school and the little boy, his 2nd grade. He really enjoyed the excitement of change enveloping him as occasioned by the move to what his mommy called "new digs." There was tremendous expectation, though short-lived, of a fresh beginning at a new school and the hope that Daddy's newly minted career would bring the family out of a rather meager lifestyle. The little boy finally had his very own bedroom with a brand-new bed and an array of new school clothes received just in time to get all spruced up for Daddy's graduation ceremonies at the police academy. Life in Tarzana started out pretty, pretty good; but it wouldn't take very long for his daddy to relentlessly resume curbing the little boy's spurts of intrepid enthusiasm.

Less than a month after the school year commenced, the little boy turned 7 years old. The whole family unit was only destined to continue, essentially unbroken, for little more than 2½ years. Although his mommy and sister E.D. tried make the best of Daddy's rather volatile temper, there was always some form of friction putting stress upon all members of the family, which by jot and tittles, gradually fractured itself to rubble. Most often, the familial stress resulted simply from the burden of witnessing Daddy's crude and haphazard treatment of his own little boy.

The transition from relative poverty to Valley life started out well enough; the family settled into the middle class as if it was their birthright. They even began to avail themselves of a luxury originally invented for the well-to-do which, by the 1950s, had become a relatively extravagant symbol of a middle-class life to be envied by the neighbors. Although a service virtually obsolete in the 21st century, the family began almost immediately receiving home delivery of milk, sundries and other products classified as "dairy", dispatched to their doorstep by 6:00 a.m., twice each week. This wasn't really much of a stretch for the family since the little boy's Grampa Freddie, had made his career as a "milkman" in Pasadena, so it was quite natural for his mommy to embrace this particular amenity for her own growing family.

Within a few short months Mommy got a great job at Rocketdyne a few miles from home in Canoga Park. She was the "secretary" (today she'd be called an executive assistant) for the head of the data processing department and by all accounts was very good at her job. Rocketdyne built engines that fitted to all the rocket ships taking our nation's astronauts into space and eventually to the Moon.

Life consisted alternatively of school, back home to do normal kid-type chores (make bed, dump trash, wash dishes, etc.), playtime afterward, then supper and some television on a 13" black and white portable, and finally bedtime. Repeat five days per week. Weekends that weren't otherwise occupied by playtime and chores were often spent at one or the other of the grandparents' homes for playtime, TV and supper. Sometimes they would make the 60-mile trek to Santa Ana (even during week nights during the summertime) to visit his daddy's "Daddy" and Gramma Beryl.

Although the facts ultimately exposed were a closely guarded secret not revealed to him for another seven years, a thorough understanding of the actual family dynamic must be disclosed here, in advance of the little boy's actual chronological awareness of the facts. The opened can of beans, when finally spilt, would morph into worms squiggling out in all directions, compelling his mind to raise more questions than available facts were sufficient in answering. Fortunately, at seven years of age, his young, tenuous brainwaves would not yet have to struggle through a very adult matter although we shall briefly do so at this time.

The little boy was 14 years old when news delivered of Gramma Beryl's death would spawn in Mommy an irrepressible compunction to reveal further grisly details previously deemed a secret to be strictly shared on a needs to know basis only. Apparently, it was her fear the family secret would be improvidently revealed to her children by some errant relative during the funeral services triggering her need to finally let the little boy know the truth of his ancestry. He was so floored by the news divulged, he later refused to attend Gramma's funeral under any circumstances.

By the time this news broke there was another matter inspiring his refusal to pay his respects to an old lady who never caused him any harm and otherwise did her level best to be a good Gramma. While life unfolded and circumstances compelled him to action, it was less than a year earlier that his daddy permitted the little boy and sister E.D. the no questions asked opportunity to cut off all ties to himself and by extension his own newly created family.

Even if the shock of the surviving "Grampa's" ancestral revelation acted as superficial motivation to eschew the funeral and sealing his intention to seek refuge in avoidance, the fact he would also have to re-immerse himself in the distasteful relationship with

Daddy is what compelled adamant rejection of joining *any* of the beings among what had become, now that the cat was out of the bag, the cretinous herd of slack-jawed cave dwellers he would certainly find attending Gramma's funeral.

His mommy began by informing him that his daddy's "Daddy" was not indeed his biological father and that his Gramma Beryl had married and divorced *another* unidentified man who actually sired the little boy's daddy. The man he had been calling "Grampa" was in fact acting the impostor all of these years.

As the tale unfolded, he was told his daddy was born with pneumonia and a little body riddled with a bullous skin disease known as pemphigus syphiliticus; the result of an infection within his mother of a ghastly case of secondary syphilis. Under the absence of proper prenatal medical care, the presence of the grotesque disease was hidden for much of his last trimester and not revealed unto Gramma Beryl or anyone else, until days just prior to the occasion of his birth. Naturally, there was an immediate split between the marriage of Beryl and the little boy's blood-Grampa.

But now the man he knew as the "Grampa" he'd always assume was his alone, became something of a dichotomy; on one hand a hero of sorts, riding in to save another little boy and his lost mommy when they needed him most, while at the same moment and on the other hand, his status as the bona fide patriarch evaporated into thin air in the mind of an impressionable teen. The young lad was torn by the news in subtle, unexplainable directions. The revelation a watershed moment wherein he developed a lifelong defense mechanism of avoiding, if not running away from confronting all things unpleasant occurring in concert with most, if not all normal, interpersonal relationships.

Upon discovering his daddy began his own life in dire circumstances, the predictable introspection ripped open the little box of secrets to the origin of his daddy's obvious hatred toward his own mother. Incidental to this unpleasant disclosure of secrets peculiar to the family's structure was instant explanation why these grandparents and especially Gramma Beryl would always strive to generously spoil their only two grandchildren.

Throughout his young life the little boy, for his part and unaware of sister E.D.'s mind on the matter, always preferred his daddy's parents over his mommy's. Essentially and probably in effort to atone for her sins against her own little boy, Gramma Beryl used her husband's considerable wherewithal to buy her grandson's loyalty to them; whereas his mommy's parents were financially incapable of even entering the competition.

Nevertheless, as the lid covering a mysterious skeleton in the family's secluded coffin lifted, the origin of conflict would eventually solidify a diaphanous comprehension into complete awareness of the nature of his dysfunction, although not necessarily achieved through the exposition of the new facts alone. Indeed, this revelation would merely serve to springboard him in the direction of a lifelong inward inquiry from whence enlightenment would grudgingly and sporadically ensue.

Although Uncle Frankie, still an airman now serving America by spinning vinyl 45's in West Germany and unable to attend the festivities; Mommy, Daddy, sister E.D. and the little boy were all invited to the Thanksgiving feast at Gramma Frances and Grampa Freddie's apartment wherein they recently settled after Aunt Caro flew from the Oneida Street nest. After dinner, Grampa Freddie excused himself not feeling well and retired to his bedroom. Within the hour he was being carried away on a gurney having suffered a massive heart attack. He would pass away in a hospital bed on November 27, 1961.

The children were deemed too young to attend the funeral so they were carted off to a friend and coworker of their daddy's for the day to be babysat the very first time by (nonprofessional) strangers outside their own family. After a relatively uneventful day playing with other people's kids, his parents returned late afternoon from the funeral to retrieve the little boy and sister E.D. for the trip home. However, rather than doing what the little boy certainly desired and calling it a day, the grownups decided to indulge everyone with pizza for supper beforehand. Although it would be the little boy's first pizza ever consumed, it would also be his first ever exposure to the gruesome mushrooms, which happened to be slathered all over the top of the damn thing.

Although to some folks they're a delicacy, the hideous presentation of thousands of blackish, icky pieces of boar boogers looked to him absolutely inedible. When *forced* to consume the strange combination of musty flavoring melded with chunky slime, mind over matter made the little boy literally wretch and refuse to complete ingestion of the concoction, now a pulpy ball of goo in his mouth. When he finally spewed it out onto his dinner plate, the retribution from Daddy was swift and sure, quite physical and again, quite public.

Thus began his lifelong abhorrence of mushrooms; curiously, pizza would somehow forever remain to him a "comfort food". Perhaps if the adults declared the stupid thing was topped with caramelized bunny eggs, he might have gobbled it up without objection; however, any vegetable lookin' food with "mush" in its name was *never* going to meet his palate's acceptance. Later, asparagus and calves' liver would suffer similar fates; although each of these foods proved both equally horrible in taste *and* texture, despite the British affinity for such obnoxious fare. No matter, he never made it easy and would always demand to be forced under threat of punishment to eat everything on his plate whenever Mommy offered these items for supper. Oh, he'd eat that crap all right, regardless how distasteful to him each item might be. However, he resented every mouthful and eventually his mommy was forced to give up trying to compel his cooperation.

For the little boy's part, the only saving grace to the beating this time around was that the family would never again socialize with these people and he would not have to face any of them ever afterward. Not only would the outburst cause the premature departure of the family from this particular social event, the argument that ensued in their car on the ride home would resurrect a recurring theme between his parents and would further serve to diminish his mommy's desire to socialize again with these folks.

The only thing of questionable value he would take away from this event was that Daddy's disciplinary technique leveled his son's direction was the primary focus of Mommy's displeasure with their marriage and she let Daddy know it in terms not ambiguous. Such would be his understanding until the day they finally divorced; that the genesis of the majority of his parent's very vocal battles centered upon Daddy's physical abuse of the little boy himself.

Perhaps the one moment in the little boy's life most frightening was the occasion, sometime in early 1962, that his daddy abandoned all pretense of self-control.

The reason for the visit to their home was neither the little boy's birthday nor his daddy's, but each of them received a gift when his daddy's "Daddy" and Gramma Beryl stopped by their Tarzana home one afternoon. It's quite possible that sister E.D. and his mommy were also presented with gifts by the grandparents that day; however, all recollection slipped away once the violence began, his daddy spun a main bearing and became completely incapable of helping himself. Instead, the adult would again focus only upon the vulnerable child in a sick effort to assuage his own unabatedly depraved inner turmoil.

Naturally, the melee did not manifest when his daddy's folks were still visiting with the family. Just as naturally, certainly in the mind's eye of a twisted adult, the allegation deemed truthful with no shadow of doubt evidenced by the fact the little boy was caught absolutely red-handed in its commission by one of "L.A.'s finest".

The fracas was focused entirely on those trinkets bestowed that day upon the males of the family by Gramma and "Grampa". Like most little boys of the era, he was a fan of many Saturday morning serial Westerns; television shows such as the *Roy Rogers Show*, *Fury* (about a spirited horse thusly named), and the *Sky*

King. As if acknowledging his appreciation of the theme, his gift from the Grams this occasion was a fancy replica cowboy suit and hat. The kind of outfit made from a satiny, khaki colored material, including a long-sleeved shirt with mother of pearl snaps instead of buttons and piping sewn into the shoulder panels and around breast pocket flaps held down by more pearly snaps and red roses embroidered above each. And, the hat, though it wasn't exactly a Stetson, it *was* a suitable replica cowboy's hat many 6- or 7-year-old boys are sure to wear at some time in his life.

Although the outfit was more in the vein of the Roy Rogers' character, with his omni-present horse Trigger, the little boy's real Saturday morning champion was instead the "Sky King" (also a Western hero with just a different kinda steed; a twin-engine Cessna). No matter, he was nevertheless convinced Gramma and "Grampa" had been reading his mind and he was thrilled to be able to dress-up like a television icon and knowing well that this gift was the kind of luxury his mommy and daddy could never afford to frivolously buy either of their two children. Suffice to say this present made for one happy little cowboy... even if only for the next hour or two.

A comfortable Pendleton Fireside button-down shirt, olive green on navy plaid with black and slender red accents, was his daddy's gift of which he too apparently held very dear. Of course, all and sundry were obliged to show the Grams how they each looked in their new duds; which both males were still wearing after the visitors left for the evening.

Thereafter and for some inexplicable reason, save the convenient excuse he was perhaps feeling a little too frisky, Daddy decided to engaged his son in a playful challenge to a wrestling match that quickly turned frightful. Almost immediately, the little boy's head became pinned underneath his daddy's chest and his ability to breath was immediately inhibited by the man's large, suffocating torso. Naturally, when the moment came, he could no longer inhale life-sustaining air; his primary instinct became focused on struggling out from under the aggressor. However, his daddy wasn't just going to let him get away that easily and he continued deliberately holding him down, cutting off the little boy's escape. Certainly, it came to the moment his conscious mind prioritized that he should free himself regardless the cost; which is precisely what the little cowboy did, spurring himself with the immediacy of instinctual self-preservation.

As the little boy's motivation increased of necessity by equal measures of fight in order to accomplish his flight, he managed to struggle free by pushing, shoving and squirming out from underneath his daddy. In doing so, the new Pendleton was torn; a relatively inconsequential 90-degree tear, one-half inch long one way and one-half inch long the other way, right where the third button down was sewn into the shirt. Given the level of retribution extended for the effrontery, the casual observer might have guessed the original trespass quite substantial; the little boy unfortunately, held an unperturbed view in conflict with this opinion.

Although the tear was evident immediately to both the little boy and his daddy equally, neither was on the same page as to the extent of the damage. Hell, he thought, he was always tearing up his clothes by just being a kid going to school and what happened to Daddy's shirt was not really anything that Mommy couldn't fix herself, toot sweet. Not only that, but given its location, the damage once repaired would never be visible or perceptible to anyone but him. Apparently, THAT wasn't the point. There was however, a message ensconced within a recurring theme the little boy would receive loud and clear... do-not-fuck-with-Daddy.

His daddy's reaction and inability to shut it all down as unbridled rage expressed; though succinct in its direction, it was otherwise quite haphazard in its application. As a fog of disbelief enveloped the little boy, the adult started to tear the child's brand-new satiny cowboy shirt right off of him, even while still draped over his little body. Utterly destroyed was the brand-new Roy Rogers outfit with the pearly snaps and the red roses embroidery, which filled a little boy with so much joy when given to him a mere 2 or 3 hours earlier.

Once the adult finished off the shirt by ripping it to shreds and pieces, he dragged the little cowboy into the kitchen and emphasized his displeasure by demonstrably throwing the stringy remnants into the trashcan. Unsatisfied at that, his daddy started on the satiny, tan-colored trousers that were part of the gifted ensemble, these too were shredded asunder and discarded along with the shirt and presumably the cowboy hat as well, since it too was never again seen after that evening.

The shit hit the fan so fast he didn't immediately ascertain whether his daddy reacted to the actual damage to the garment or a child's cavalier attitude; there simply was no time in his young life to even be aware of the distinction, much less evaluate the impetus for such extreme behavior. Bewildered and left with nothing more than piss-filled jockey shorts and the certain knowledge he would be going to bed without the supper Mommy was cooking for them when the grudge match began, the little boy was now in no mood to try and figure out what made his daddy go so totally berserk.

Instead, and stripped of all dignity in the darkness of that lonely bedroom, the little boy, having lost his prized new uniform, would begin a long ride toward a personality disorder called "borderline", before slumber slowly replaced reality for dreamland.

Having had much of his errant hyperactivity usually possessed at home knocked out of him by now; the little boy began 2nd grade trying to keep a low profile at school. Unfortunately, there was an incident before the Thanksgiving holiday break in which he was accused of punching a classmate over a lunchtime food-exchanging bargain gone sour. An examination of fault was apparently deemed irrelevant; suffice to say the little boy did not get the better of the deal and had to take blame for all of it, including a false accusation…the striking of a little girl!

In fact, there was a lesson to be learned here that under such matters of boy against girl, the grownups didn't give a shit at all in examining who was at fault...*he* was at fault; period. Once he supposedly struck her, all other discussion ceased and judgment summarily issued; ownership of the only course of action left being his alone, including whatever corrective retribution was deemed sufficient reinforcement of the point.

Ordinarily the little boy brought a sack lunch his mommy prepared for him to school every day, excepting each and every Friday when Mommy gave he and sister E.D. 50-cents each to buy lunch that day from the school cafeteria. Even though the incident with little Mary T. Cookie-Thief occurred mid-week, the little boy would never again share anything that came out of either that lunch sack or off the cafeteria's plastic tray. Nevermore would sister E.D., nor even his best school chums, be allowed to pry, cajole or barter the contents of the lunch *he* was supposed to be eating.

Regrettably, the incident having occurred so near the beginning of the school year as it did simultaneously serve to negatively announce his presence and permanently impacted the rest of his classmates' attitude toward him. Moreover, and for his part, the incident left such a bad taste in his mouth for the embarrassment of now being known and identified as *that boy* who beat up little Mary, he could envision never going to school again a completely reasonable remedy.

Fortunately for the little boy, the fact his daddy was this day otherwise occupied at work compelled a punishment that would necessarily defer to Mommy's discretion; who summarily and unilaterally administered a traditional spanking that afternoon after returning from the parent/teacher soirée caused by his act of baseless impudence. Although the intensity of correction was halfhearted by alternative comparison, *her* resulting embarrassment would predictably compel the de rigueur bedroom banishment; early bedtime and provisionally, he would eat no supper that evening.

One day, some while before the lunchtime fiasco, something happened to him that carried with it a freaky dichotomy disguised at once as soothing catharsis, which all too soon became a self-debilitating crutch. As if occupying two sides of the same coin, the relief seemed naturally hardwired into a very real human necessity on one side, while the other side of this particular coin was not so kind. When rank gratification supplanted self-control, what was once an effective defense mechanism eventually transformed into the root of infirmity that stunted his growth into the whole measure of well-adjusted manhood and into a being possessed of a healthy personality maturing compatibly with the coincidental expansion of his physical presence.

The occasion compelling the little boy's aimless wandering about the neighborhood began as innocently; just as any normal 7-year-old male child with nothing better to do should greet a beautiful spring-like Saturday morning. There was no rhyme or reason for the contest to begin with, but at some point in time he decided to test his climbing skills, of which he was always quite proud and might be found at any random interval climbing up any tree that looked climbable. Indeed, the power line tower in the accessible DWP field down the street was a veritable jungle gym on steroids and a favorite place for the little boy to get way, waaaay above the crowd. His irrepressibility in this regard seemed to reveal a little boy born possibly with one or two strands of naturally occurring monkey DNA.

For no particular reason, the little boy set sights upon one of those steel poles cemented into the sidewalk at almost every neighborhood intersection citywide. Just then, one of those pieces of 2" diameter pipe, about 10 feet tall that supported a city-designated metal street sign was exactly what he needed to convert an impulsive notion into a bona fide challenge gratifying the little boy's competitive spirit, especially since there was no one else around with whom to play.

If gratifying his immediate needs were indeed his goal, the result of this particular decision would surely redefine the term. As the little boy shinnied up the street signpost be began to experience in his groin, under his trousers... some very unusual, yet not

entirely unpleas...wait, wait... uh-oh..., wait..., ..., uh, uh...,
.... Whoa; th-that wasn't t-too bad; n-not too bad a-a-a-at
all. Almost immediately thereafter he slid down the pole to the
sidewalk below, spent but otherwise quite enlightened.

Even at the tender age of 7-years, his little penis had its first
orgasm right there and then, on that very street corner, just 100 feet
from his front porch and unashamedly in front of anyone passing
by who happened to witness all the squirming. Being nowhere near
puberty, there was nothing "biological" deposited in the little boy's
jockey shorts, but shiver and shake he did while writhing at the top
of the pole and grasping the sign marking the intersection of
Collins St. at Crebs Avenue. The fact that he could knock his own
socks off in sexual ecstasy came as a complete and predictably, not
an unwelcome surprise. Shortly after this experience came the
really bad part; he found out that he could repeat the sensation
virtually at will. And repeat it he did, again and again and again.

Regardless of the effectiveness of the new-found catharsis
and the instant gratification it provided, it would not take long for
him to receive the message that what he was doing was not only
manifestly negative behavior, it was also definitely not something
a little boy should do in class and in front of fellow classmates.
Sadly, this message he only garnered after frustration got the better
part of his self-control. Initially however, the little boy was very
careful to never reveal this secret new game of self-abuse to
another soul.

That is... not until the dynamics of the matter in which he
supposedly beat hell out of Mary T. Cookie-Thief ran headlong
into a little boy's building frustration caused by the unrequited
annoyance of being given no proper hearing *and* having the
entirety of blame for the incident being hoisted solely upon his
shoulders. Although this lunchtime cookie bartering business
turned ugly was an isolated incident, the response from the adults
in charge at his school seemed to him just a continuum of the hell
he was living every day at home and out of range of outside
scrutiny.

Even more injustice was surrounding him at school for which this incident only served to produce additional evidence that, no matter what, he was to blame for the occurrence of every bad thing. He took the blame and the brunt of the abuse when the glass pane sliced his arm, even though sister E.D. closed the door as he pushed it opened; it was he who must have been responsible for his parents separation, since he had to nearly die to get them reunited; when *all* the kids were teasing Conrad the biker, the little boy took sole punishment for the sins of the group; when Bradley sliced a stranger's car tire, his parents believed the cops; when he went up the street to return the errant postcard, he was to blame even though he was doing what his mommy told him to do. And now... when he was only trying to defend his sack lunch brought special from home, yet nobody believed *him* even though he told all the adults the God's honest truth of his innocence.

It wasn't the cookie robbery incident that alone triggered his secret to finally exhibit itself publicly. That occasion would occur the next morning at about 9 o'clock when he was in the middle of a handwriting lesson in which the whole class was repeating practice techniques for the art of applying cursive writing to a sheet of paper.

The written word being the natural extension of the learning experience, the little boy earlier mastered the art of *printing* words very quickly and even excelled at it without too much difficulty. However, due of the extent of the earlier injuries to his right and dominant arm and the consistent manner in which his pencil must be held to write legibly in cursive form, the effort became a tremendous physical struggle for him. Having the difficulty as he did with his hand and arm coordination, which inexplicably decoupled from his brain's ability to issue the correct operating commands, the little boy struggled mightily at keeping pace with the rest of his classmates. Not only were his motor skills all screwed up and the movements and strokes impossible to repeat with any consistency, the calisthenics required of his right arm were so excruciatingly painful that doing such a difficult task caused his hand and arm to ache long after the activity ceased.

Normally a very good student, he was a quick witted and thoughtful little boy who grasped most things quite readily. Except this cursive writing bullshit would become to him a frustrating obstacle, but not a lifelong, insurmountable one. The simmering of vexation was the occasion when a frustrated little boy vainly attempted laying down repeating groups of squiggles onto a piece of doublewide line paper in a manner generally resembling other squiggles, as authorized by academia. Regardless that he was applying the full extent of his physical effort, he simply could not do the exercises with any legible level of consistency.

Relatively speaking, there wasn't a 7-year-old child alive in 1961 middle class America that knew much of anything at all about sex; sadly, the same thing can definitely not be said these days. Nevertheless, this little boy didn't have a clue and didn't know the difference then between sex and socks. So, when he masturbated, he didn't grab himself and simulate the sex act, he was simulating a steel pole and the act of rubbing oneself along it as he shinnied up the damn thing. Indeed, he wasn't even really "jerking off" per sé; he wouldn't learn of such techniques of simulating sex acts with his hand for many years down the road. For now, he would just rub himself with his knuckles, over his trousers and underpants, furiously for about 20 seconds and poof… if his boiling internal frustration was not entirely eliminated, it was certainly alleviated, if only temporarily.

When the little boy finally had enough of trying and failing to complete the handwriting lessons expected, he sort of just scooted himself a little farther underneath his desk and proceeded to furiously rubbing his penis right there in the classroom. Certainly, and even if he did attempt to maintain some measure of discretion under the circumstances, there could be no doubt that his monkeyshines did not go unnoticed by some, if not the whole class. At this point and even if someone did notice, it would not have mattered much; the urge was entirely irrepressible. Did he get busted over this incident? Of course, he did; the behavior was a holdover from the previous day's discipline and the school officials were all over him like stink on feces. Fuck…how would he ever find words to explain this?

There can be no doubt that his parents were absolutely struck by disbelief at the notion that the little boy was behaving as he was for purposes of achieving an orgasm. "No, that can't be what he's doing, is it?" Even though they wanted to get to the bottom of his behavior, they did nothing more than tap-dance all around their burning curiosity. Sure, they made demands to know *why* he was doing it, but never actually asking *what* it was that he was really doing under those pants of his. He volunteered nothing, clammed up tight and wouldn't say squat didley. Repeatedly they pressed; "What's going on? Do you have an itch? Are your pants too tight?" On and on they continued harping at him, while he only gave 'em back bupkis.

Initially, he was certain the jig was up and he would not be able to continue implementing his special curative while anyone else also knew of his antics. More than anything, the questions his parents pressed on him were uncomfortably close to the reality they refused to believe in the first place; that what he was doing indeed resulted in he getting his rocks knocked right off.

In other words, while somehow garnering an understanding that except for his extreme youth, they may have otherwise been on to his actual shenanigans and by admitting to the truth would cause his parents to somehow enforce the cessation of the only satisfying thing in his life. For sure, he must immediately discontinue the practice of frantic, hi-speed dick rubbing anywhere else but in strictest privacy lest he elicit more questions from Mommy and Daddy certain to eventually break his wavering ability to obfuscate.

Then suddenly he got lucky. Just as soon as he ran plum out of excuses, they seemingly dismissed his behavior as anything sexually related; providence stepped in and the matter was a subject mysteriously closed forever. The whole matter concluded when Mommy and Daddy bought the little boy new pants and new jockey shorts a size larger than necessary and that was the end of that.

Nevertheless, he couldn't risk a close call like this one again, especially if he wanted to hold on tightly to this particularly screwy, yet quite effective security blanket. At the most basic level of examination the little boy would view himself all through 2nd grade as a friendless outcast and loner. Beating a girl classmate early in the semester and beating his meat later in the classroom didn't really endear him to the others and he was mindful of the dismal reality and the fact only he was responsible for bringing this shit upon himself.

Through a mindset gelled fairly opaque, it seemed clear he was the target of a personal attack one day at morning recess when his right thumb "collapsed" in dire pain after becoming severely dislocated from its socket. Regardless of the actual nature of the assault, he would for the rest of the school year believe his little hand was struck by the volleyball thrown at his back in a deliberately antagonistic act by a classmate while he drank from the water fountain in the lunchroom. Of course, his immediate reaction was to bolt from the drinking fountain while screaming, "My thumb's collapsed, my thumb's collapsed" and sprinting desperately to the nurse's office seeking first aid.

He would finish the 2nd grade without a significant friend and leave with only untrustworthy acquaintances.

In effort to socialize a rather shy and withdrawn little boy, his parents signed him up for the Cub Scouts at the beginning of summer break from school. Their belief seemed to be that he should follow in his daddy's footsteps on his own path to manhood. Again, he would resist this activity at first, much like nursery school, but after a short while he really began to enjoy most of the scouting experience.

Since he supposedly also had a cousin somewhere who

brought pride to the family name as some kind of record setting Eagle (Boy) Scout, the little boy at first aspired to be inspirational to his own mommy and daddy, as well. Years later, when Mark Spitz made winning 7 Olympic Gold Medals look easy as making cake, the little boy would determine to bring similar glory to the family, himself a would-be Olympic medalist. He would realize neither aspiration; in fact, as to Cub Scouts, he never even made it to the "Webelo" ranks and his swimming career never made it past the first week of high school tryouts. Although he always enjoyed various intellectual pursuits, while he was still a little boy, he would never enthusiastically embrace much intense physical rigor and his attention span for things of no interest to him was exceptionally limited.

In general, the little boy's scouting experience was positive for he basically rode his daddy's coattails in many of the required activities. It seems his daddy was quite the hobbyist model maker as well as a seasoned Scout from the years before his military service and in this case, if anyone was really having fun being a Cub Scout, it was more his daddy than it was the little boy. As a result, he earned many of his merit badges on the back of a man who (as a cop) was little more than a professional Boy Scout himself. Indeed, Daddy ascended far beyond the Webelos and even a mere Boy Scout; in fact, his daddy participated extensively in the Sea Scout program preparatory to joining the U.S. Navy.

One benefit for the little boy in joining this particular Cub Scout troop was the fact that none of the kids his age went to Tarzana Elementary. All the boys in this troop were either older than he or went to other schools, so the fact he didn't really fit in at his own school and mesh well with those kids was not a distraction that might otherwise have inhibited his wholehearted participation. So, he did the best he could and the fact that his daddy brought so much to the Scouting table really allowed the little boy to cruise through the experience and in some cases excel beyond some of the other boys; his daddy lubricating the skids, one merit badge at a time.

Yes, he was hoisted through his scouting experience on the back of his daddy; yet, there was indeed a lot the little boy would learn simply from observing how his daddy accomplished the various tasks that were beyond the little boy's skill, but right up his daddy's alley. The entire scouting experience with his daddy effectively sowed fertile seeds of mechanical ability within the little boy that continually bear fruit more than five decades later.

Of course, the specter that hell could rain down upon him suddenly and anytime Daddy became pissed (à la, the earlier "Conrad incident") always haunted the little boy during any scouting activity in which Daddy also participated. That fear was good cause to discourage his desire to become a Cub Scout initially, and yet because he was apparently being coaxed into walking in his daddy's footprints, he was powerless to escape this new association.

Luckily for the little boy, the onetime his daddy's temper finally did flare-up publicly at a weekend campout at a Palm Desert, California Cub Scout retreat, it was all the *other* kids (this time) whom were forced to endure his bizarre outrage. For his part in the matter, the little boy was either deemed entirely blameless of offense or was somehow made otherwise invisible to his daddy throughout an ordeal all the other boys would have to suffer, while he skated away totally unmolested. Remaining unscathed and grateful for a minor miracle that evening, the little boy experienced an intensity of relief once the fury finally passed, in which he settled into his own sleeping bag the only kid in the room who didn't have to clean the crap out of his pants before turning in for the night.

Chapter 4

*T*o whatever measure the little boy's daddy determined to make him a Scout, his Mommy was equally keen upon making him a God-fearing one at that. Scout Law demands the adherent to always be trustworthy, loyal, helpful, friendly, courteous, kind, obedient, cheerful, thrifty, brave, clean, and reverent and damn it; Mommy was going to ensure his reverence to Christian priorities above all else. Although both children were born and baptized into the Roman Catholic faith, it was not until the move to Tarzana at which time some unexplained motivation compelled their mommy to begin regular attendance at Our Lady of Grace Catholic diocese on Ventura Boulevard in Encino. Excepting their daddy, the family attended Mass every Sunday; including several hours on several consecutive Saturdays during the little boy's 8th summer, which were dedicated to Catechism classes for both children preparatory to each being allowed to receive Holy Communion. The year was 1962.

Getting a haircut was always an unpleasant ordeal. The little boy hated both the process and the way he looked afterward. The fact that his parents forced him to sport a "flat-top" style haircut was a big part of the problem and even more so once the Beatles came into his sphere of awareness. Why he couldn't just look like a normal boy and must look like a sailor enlisted in the Navy was never explained and he would be forced to look like a dork until high school, primarily at his mommy's insistence. The little boy would forever find the peculiar human activity and its necessary regularity an entirely odious experience; and the creepy men to which his mommy took him called barbers, with their stupid dirty jokes didn't help matters, either. Of course, he never cared for the necessity of defecating, washing the dinner dishes, or doing laundry, either... Nevertheless, in matters such as these, he pretty much resigned himself to whatever fate happened to be in the cards dealt each and every day.

With his daddy's influence came the pragmatic, his mommy's influence the ethereal and his conscious self would begin a transformation of which he became all too aware. Essentially a momma's boy (whose self-identity thus far meshed easily with a mostly gentle and loving mother), he would begin to acquire very scary knowledge of the reality of his own independence as a human being (soon to be a man just like his daddy) living on Earth. Unfortunately, his daddy's immaturity and lack of self-control, coupled with a mommy only capable of intervening after the fact, fostered within every fiber of his being a confusion only just beginning to undermine a fragile self-esteem.

It was always when time intersected his daddy's varying perception of the child's misdeeds (committed innocently enough) that the little boy's personal focus would invariably lament such new-found understanding of his own human-ness; inquiring inward after each father/son conflict something akin to, "why does this happen to me?"

Such internal doubts were prevalent aspects of his life until one summer evening when the reality of living in a big city collided with what was slowly becoming an underlying, yet pervasive fear of his daddy's temper; where even his mere presence at home during off-duty hours instilled in the little boy a bewildering trepidation. If he had learned anything by now it was that his daddy could be one mean son of a bitch when dealing with an errant little boy. What he would soon discover was a daddy who could be quite the badass whenever a stranger got too close and invaded the family's space, too.

Essentially, the little boy's private reality became far more warped as self-doubt welded to a seemingly justifiable self-loathing. This was the time in his life when the little boy's personality would set itself in stone; integrating within his soul an identity with dreadful roots out of which he would never seem able to grow. In spite of his conscious awareness of its heinousness, and regardless how much he wished it weren't so, this little apple fell to the base of the tree and stayed there a lifetime. If only a caterpillar came along and devoured him he might someday soar away in the innards of a transmogrified Tiger Swallowtail... no; he was and always would be akin to that man's ilk.

Along with expressions of intolerance toward virtually all people of all stripes and repeated exhibitions of road rage hurled whenever he became displeased with another driver on the Valley's byways, the little boy not only came to loathe the man, he moreover came to loathe the fact that he too was undeniably chipped from identical stock. Try as he might, through the years of his youth and beyond, to resist adopting a similar outward behavior, he was nonetheless influenced by one bad example after another in observing his daddy's expressions of internal rage. He too was forever susceptible under times of stress to regress harmfully toward these earliest of learned experiences.

Regardless of lifelong efforts to suppress the truth, whenever the shit hit the fan of personalities tenuously yoked by relationship, his automatic and immediate response would usually manifest into an inner rage over which he would manage varying degrees of control. Sadly, when rage supplanted control and his only prudent course of action was to flee, his reactions would be branded by others as cowardice rather than given any credence as valorous discretion, which at times always remained the motivation at heart.

For more reason than one, he was forbidden to allow rage an outlet of expression, at least as regards immediately addressing the source of any conflict. Maybe there were means and methods for dealing with human obstacles, but he was not learning these things from either parent. The little bastard's only relief would quickly be found at his earliest opportunity for a little privacy when the knuckles of his right hand would immediately begin to fiercely rub at his dick under his corduroy trousers for 30 or 40 seconds until his frustration would evaporate in a blessed orgasm. However wrong it was (and it **was**) for the little boy to express himself in this manner, at least he had something with which to vent unrequited torment. Fortunately, and for the time being, this particular pressure relief mechanism kept him out of jail all during his youth; though soon after the beginning of his third decade jail time would become more inevitable, as even normal sex in abundance couldn't alleviate his formidable anguish.

To his daddy's credit, what the man lacked in education was compensated through thoughtful application of sheer brainpower; however, what he lacked in patience he gladly replaced with an unabashed ability to walk away from a task unfinished without worrying too much about being called a quitter.

Naturally, the little boy would assimilate and adopt all of these characteristics and to one degree or another, many of his daddy's bad habits would soon become his own and there was simply nothing he could do to about it. This one thing... the fact that he was his daddy's son and deep down held his daddy's anger as his own... would haunt him for a lifetime; therapy-schmerapy. It wasn't so much that he willingly embraced the roots of hatred; rather, by osmosis these things were slowly beaten into him via experiential psychology usually accompanied by corporal reinforcement.

There came a time not too long into his daddy's second year as an L.A. cop that the little boy (who loathed it when Daddy was at home and not otherwise occupied with his cop work) was faced with a situation after which he would be forever grateful his daddy *was* a cop and indeed, *was at home* on the evening the whole shitstorm went down. An incident that serendipitously occurred right under the nose (.38 snubnose revolver, that is) of a bona fide L.A.P.D. policeman, which frightened the little boy just short of soiling his P.J.'s.

Upon later reflection, it would not be lost on him that this incident could have occurred to just Mommy and the kids without the aid of their strong daddy being there to lend help at the time. Shit, to think about what might have happened to them in that case? Somehow the little boy knew instinctively that things might have otherwise gone very badly that night.

The occasion was a late afternoon daytrip to Daddy's parent's house to show them the new car they had just that day purchased for their son; it being a gift promised if and when he should graduate from the police academy *and* maintain L.A.P.D. employment for at least a year. He had his heart set on a new 1962 Chevy Corvair "Monza", the super-zoot, 2-door model of what would soon turn into being a pretty crappy car with a bad reputation. In a color not exactly red and not a burgundy either, it had black vinyl bucket seats, a manual 4-speed transmission and an inherent unreliability completely masked by its apparent sportiness. All that mattered at the time was that it was a cool car and his daddy spent all that earlier morning negotiating a deal with a downtown Chevy dealer just down the hill from Dodger Stadium, which catered to the cops graduating from their neighboring L.A. Police Academy.

Even though it was his daddy who negotiated the deal, it was with a check signed by the little boy's "Grampa" by which it was a sealed deal. Naturally, his daddy was obligated that evening to drive the vehicle the 60-odd miles from the San Fernando Valley on down to Santa Ana; partly to express his gratitude to his folks and partly to show-off his young family and their sporty new ride to all and sundry passing by.

It was curious (but not yet known to him that his "Grampa" was actually an impostor) why his daddy secretly held so much anger and obvious hatred for his own mommy, but not nearly any at all for "Grampa". And yet, despite Daddy's disdain for his own mommy, the little boy never wondered for a minute why it was such a closely guarded secret; after all, Gramma was the wife of the moneybags making possible all things like a shiny new car. Repeatedly and predictably, his daddy would tap the source time and again whenever opportunity was ripe for taking a draught from the well belonging to the little boy's pliant "Grampa". Hypocrisy? Perhaps; nevertheless, none of it was lost at all on the observant little boy.

And so, on a beautiful breezy evening about 6:30, early in June just after school let out for the summer, the kids were instructed before leaving to put on their pajamas since they'd be returning well past their bedtime and would assuredly zonk-out on the ride back home, if not beforehand. This way, once they all returned to their house, the folks wouldn't have to fuss with the kids and (being pre-p.j.'d) could thusly shuffle them off to bed easy-squeezy.

More than the others, it was the little boy so totally excited about the new car and this trip to Gramma 'n "Grampa's" house, that he *had* to be the first to climb inside the sweetest ride in the neighborhood. When his mommy finally signaled that he could leave the house for the trip, the little boy bolted through the front door and ran down the pathway through the front yard. When he reached the corner of the house where the garage attached, he turned right to the driveway to the badass new car sporting the white gear shift knob (on which the shifting pattern was embossed in black) that he couldn't wait to paw and imagine one day he would learn how to operate just like an adult. Except this time the little boy didn't exactly obtain the gratification he thoroughly anticipated once he reached the car.

Due to his exuberance and desire to be first to get to the car, nobody else in the family actually witnessed the sight that so frightened the little boy and caused him to retreat back to the front porch screaming to anyone who would listen; "there's a dead man in the car, there's a dead man in the car". What no one else saw when the little boy opened the passenger door was a vagrant sleeping in the backseat with an arm resting awkwardly against the interior door panel that, once opened, flopped out of the car and toward the little boy so fast and limp he thought for sure this guy was stone-cold dead.

Of course, his parents would ignore the alarm raised, perhaps because of the absurdity of the claim or maybe it was the shrillness of the delivery that generated disbelief; nevertheless, while the little boy was seeking refuge in the house his parents and sister E.D. continued strolling out to the car without a care in the world, oblivious to the cause of the little boy's fright. After a minute or two and with no one returning to fetch him, the little boy ventured outside to find not the dead man he was certain of, but some snaggle-toothed old guy blabbering in Spanish and resisting Daddy's effort to attach hand cuffs to his wrists while his mommy nervously pointed Daddy's 2-inch Smith in the general area of a stranger's head absent proper tonsorial management.

Once the cuffs were on the man, Mommy gave up the gun and went inside to call the cops. Very soon a couple of officers from the West Valley division arrested the vagabond on an outstanding warrant and a charge of vagrancy. They didn't even wait for the prisoner-laden patrol car to pull away from the curb in front of their house before the family piled into the little steel cracker box and motored, albeit tardily, to Santa Ana for the rest of the evening.

After they arrived safely at Gramma 'n "Grampa's" home, the kids settled in to watching the *Red Skelton* television show on the color Magnavox in the den while some vague tension seemed to be bristling between the little boy's daddy and Gramma Beryl in the kitchen. As usual and in spite of the conflict, the adults all sat around the kitchen table boisterously throwing the dice and yelling Yahtzee until the kids (as predicted) slumbered on the sofa under the glow of the color cathode ray tube emanating from the corner of the room.

The family returned sometime past midnight; with the kids staying sound asleep on the Monza's safety-belt-less rear bench seat the whole way home. After all the excitement earlier in the evening and considering the degree of fear he experienced at the onset, the little boy (once settled comfortably into bed early that morning) was confident in the knowledge his daddy was there too, that he had a gun and that he knew also how to use it effectively. It also helped comfort the little boy that his daddy had friends at the police department who would spring quickly into action to help a fellow police officer in need.

The next morning brought a day of reflection to the little boy from which he made an unsettling observation not immediately comprehended by an exhausted child. The annoyance stemmed from a comment his daddy made as soon as the little Chevy pulled away from the curb in departing from Gramma 'n "Grampa's" home. Despite the offhandedness of his remark and with the little boy's immediate comprehension stalled until the next day, when the memory fully recovered soon after he awoke the recollection was quite vivid. As Daddy started driving the car away from the curb in front of his parent's house, he told Mommy in disgust, that if he "ever caught that bitch driving down an L.A. city street", he would use whatever means necessary to make certain he wrote her a traffic ticket.

God... how his daddy, yesterday's hero, could be such an asshole!

To be fair, having an L.A. cop for a daddy had its perks. Once, the family went to Disneyland and while riding on the Mark Twain Riverboat attraction in Frontierland, his daddy pulled whatever strings were necessary (i.e., he flashed his cop badge) to allow the family to ride around Tom Sawyer's Island... in the paddleboat's *wheelhouse* and with official Disneyland *certificates* attesting to the fact the children were each named an honorary Captain for the trip. Yeah, they designated sister E.D. a Captain too; giving both kids each an official document as proof.

Of course, they argued all the way home and for much of the next week about which one of them got to steer the boat longer. The little boy never did accept E.D.'s assertion that the ride operator let her drive the enormous boat around the island longer than allowed of him. Of course, in reality, the paddleboat is guided around the island entirely via a track mechanism and the only true function of the "wheelhouse" is simply to offer the highest vantage point on the attraction; and to give some lucky little kids harmless thrills by simulating an activity of great responsibility usually reserved for adults.

Although the children weren't entirely the architects of their summer itinerary, any latitude they may have enjoyed was found in their being allowed to make their own choice in whatever afternoon matinee they would catch at the Corbin Theater; to which sister E.D. and the little boy walked pretty much every Saturday morning whenever not otherwise occupied by their parents' wishes.

One of those parental requisites included, during the earliest weeks of that summer, the extensive training of the kids as expert swimmers. Since their daddy was a certifiable water rat and had every intention himself of participating in various forms of water sports as his expanding fortunes would allow, if the family was also going to play along with him, precautions to eliminate the possibility of drowning the children in the process were given top priority.

His daddy was so serious about the matter he became an American Red Cross certified swimming instructor and during a vacation from police work taught a class of a dozen or so other children, along with his own two, over a four-week period at a nearby public swimming pool. Both of his children took to the water as naturally as baby sea turtles lucky enough to make it to water's edge and not plucked from earth by a scavenging gull before getting there. The little boy showed tremendous heart at pleasing his daddy by giving the effort all of his attentiveness and determination. Both children, if not the whole class, all became Red Cross credentialed swimmers that summer.

Swimming instruction was fundamentally important that summer for two other reasons; the family would very often be visiting Daddy's "uncle" Gus, who owned a nicely appointed, four-bedroom house in nearby Reseda. Additionally, both children would have to spend a good deal of time during the week at a day camp in Northridge because of their parent's erratic work schedule. Each of these locations had a swimming pool the kids would be essentially compelled to use and their parents, especially Daddy, were nothing if not obsessively safety conscious when it came to all water related activities.

One of his daddy's personality traits the little boy assumed himself early in life was this notion of safety first and the behavior manifest itself in a curious way that summer. It all began with the televised influence of U.S. government propaganda commercials featuring Smokey the Bear, the famous bear cub saved by firefighters after his mommy bear died in a forest fire. Although somewhat fictionalized, the little boy would find inspiration in the efforts of the anti-wildfire crusader starring in TV shows and public service announcements in between the *Mousketeers* and *Howdy Doody*.

However, with no opportunities readily available to stare down spontaneous blazes springing up randomly in the neighborhood, the little boy soon identified a suitable alternative community hazard in need of his services as officer Smokey the safety boy. What with the tremendous quantity of broken glass strewn all over the sidewalk down the street and running along Wilbur Avenue just underneath the freeway overpass a block from home, something must be done about these dangerous obstacles and it appeared left to him to handle the undertaking.

Whenever he and sister E.D. would walk down Wilbur to Ventura Boulevard and say... head over to Jake's Jug liquor store on an errand with a note from Mommy giving them permission to buy for her a pack of Kent filters; once they arrived at the overpass, the little boy self-identifying as Smokey, would go ahead of his sister to clear the pathway of any shards of broken glass he found on the sidewalk.

The reason there was so much broken glass present was due to the nature of the overpass and its concrete walls that beckoned glass smashing from any passing riff-raff with an empty beer or Coke bottle in hand. Under these circumstances there would forever be an abundance of work to be done and since he *was* Smokey the safety boy that summer, his little sister would never have to fear being mortally gashed as he nearly was only a few years earlier.

The little boy's participation at the Northridge day camp was for him more a chore than enjoyable and was really nothing more than activity-centric gang babysitting. The other kids were obnoxious little brats, the old lady running the place was worse than Mrs. Ness in his estimation and he would be forever grateful when it was no longer necessary to attend. Uncle Gus's house and swimming pool, on the other hand, was a different matter.

The spacious house on Kittridge Street in Reseda was a palace of utter solace for the little boy. For one thing, the other kids there were mostly family; but moreover, the place was a sanctuary of sorts mainly due to the respect his daddy had for his "uncle." Maybe it wasn't as much respect as it was the fear of discovery for who and what he really was. Regardless of reason, Daddy was always very careful anytime his children required discipline whenever visiting with Uncle Gus's family and the little boy never hesitated to bask in the safety of this apparent refuge when it was made available to him.

As near as he was ever able to pin the matter, the little boy believed Uncle Gus was married to one of Gramma Beryl's relatives but exactly how that relation connected was never disclosed or discussed. All the little boy really knew was that Uncle Gus was a Captain with the Los Angeles County Fire department and moonlighted out of his garage in Reseda as an upholsterer. Gus made a pretty good living for himself, sired three attractive teenage daughters and provided a very nice home for his family, which he generously shared with his "nephew."

The biggest surprise that summer was a camping trip to Refugio Beach State Park on the coast of California, north/west of

Santa Barbara. They would borrow Uncle Gus's pickup truck and camper and the whole family, including Coco their toy poodle, would spend an idylic week at the beach. Their daddy would bring along his SCUBA diving gear and they would eat barbequed, freshly harvested abalone and roast marshmallows over a campfire. It was going to be bitchen.

Everything about that trip excelled, except (of course) the abalone, which was like eating crap flavored leather; but regardless of that unpleasantness, another incident flared totally out of control by the seemingly well-meaning actions of a complete madman. Notwithstanding good intentions, the scar left behind was from a cut mangling everything deeper than skin battle-hardened by previous physical abuse; this time every fiber of any remaining trust the little boy begrudged his daddy would be forever and inexorably altered as was the gossamer fabric of his future emotional stability. It all began, as everything the little boy did that invariably got him into some sort of unintended trouble, when he stepped out of his comfort zone while reaching for some measure of his own independence.

Saturday would be the last full day the family's itinerary had scheduled for the beach side vacation and related merriment. On Friday morning the little boy's daddy would do something apparently timed for maximum effect and accomplished when the beach area was the center of attention for the majority of campers and visitors at the park that day.

Not only were all the children on the beach abuzz with what he was about to do, the hubbub alerted all and sundry on the beach that a man was about to do what only Mike Nelson (from TV's "Sea Hunt") could do, right there on this very beach. It was true that it was his daddy doing this thing and it was also true he was the only kid on the beach with a daddy who *could* even do such a thing. The experience filled him with tremendous pride and a surprising self-confidence, which enveloped him for the next day and a half. Although commonplace today, in 1962 no one ever heard of Jacques Yves Cousteau and very few people even had the desire to learn to SCUBA dive, much less having the wherewithal to make such a thing happen.

For a short while he was the son of that man who came up the beach from the sea bearing a net bag filled with icky delicacies and the whole episode instilled in the little boy a certain measure of hubris and a bit of a swollen head.

On Saturday morning he managed to fortify himself in the previous day's past glory mustering the courage to steal a kiss from a little girl with whom he had been hanging around on the park's jungle gym. It wasn't a matter of him just upping and molesting a perfect stranger; indeed, for the past couple of days this particular little girl had been the object of considerable attention from the little boy and a temporary chum who had been there most of the week as well, camping with his own family. This other boy and his family were from Reseda, and the prospective sweetheart? A mystery. Then whoof... as if only diaphanous memory, the little girl soon disappeared once the little boy executed his stealthy and boldly amorous acrobatics. Apparently, it was an advance unwelcomed.

The sweet life turned ugly that evening after supper, when the little boy took sister E.D. over to the bluffs where the beach ended and the not beach part of the park began. Things turned almost immediately sour when he thought he should be accepted among some teenagers whom were playing with an enormous inner tube and rolling down the bluff inside the tube's center opening. It is not clear how the incident occurred but the result was the little boy soon had both his eyelids filled with coarse beach sand and through the grating pain became certain he would be forever blinded. Thankfully, sister E.D. managed to help him return for most necessary first aid to Uncle Gus's camper, where his mommy and daddy were engrossed this evening playing the always popular game 'o Yahtzee. Regrettably, the adult Sea Scout immediately sprang into action to alleviate his troubled son's agony and fear.

Except the adult didn't have a clue what he should do to repair matters. Maybe the little boy's panic was contagious and he brain farted, who knows? Rather than trying to do the reasonable thing and use the faucet to flush his eyes out, his daddy resorted to rank idiocy. The man's immediate reaction and the strategy he foolishly and doggedly adopted until it finally worked was to try to compel the little boy to *manufacture* his own tears to flush the foreign matter from his eyes.

Unfortunately, the motivation his daddy initially selected to cause the little boy to cry didn't have the desired effect at first and he was forced to further improvise. To make something clear before advancing through this episode, once he became a cop with license to carry a handgun anywhere, his daddy was *never* without either the snubnose .38 Smith or a Colt Model 1911 .45 auto, in a holster and at his side. Of course, his service revolver was a 6-inch Smith & Wesson .38 Special, the most powerful handgun L.A.P.D. allowed their officers to use in the field at the time.

Becoming entirely befuddled by his son's wholesale un-cooperation, the policeman daddy did absolutely the most unthinkable thing, but did so in such a manner to everybody present while demonstrating a most convincing intention of purpose. Before putting the cap on his sincerity, he made it quite clear that if the little boy didn't shape-up, he would make poor little Coco the poodle pay the ultimate price for *the lad's inability to properly behave in life.*

And with that, his daddy grabbed the .38 snubber in his right hand and the helpless chocolate-colored dog by the scruff of his neck with the left; then he put the gun to the little dog's head and threatened to take him there and then up above the bluffs and blow his little brains out. If the little boy didn't start behaving correctly and do it pretty damn soon, killing his dog was exactly what this old bastard was going to do, **goddammit**.

Ultimately, Coco dodged a bullet that evening and the little boy's tears did finally flush out the painfully offending sand, but the trust lost that night would be gone forever and for all his years remaining. This incident alone cemented a developing schizophrenic "respect" for his father. On the one hand he was developing a qualified fear of his daddy while he was away from home because his absence made the little boy feel vulnerable to possible exposure to the criminal element, like the vagabond he found that night sleeping in backseat of their Monza; while on the other hand, the little boy harbored an unqualified fear, bordering on dread, of the man whenever he was present in the home, essentially for the very same reason.

Chapter 5

*T*hird grade began as if the summer's heat had boiled away his sordid past from 2nd grade and the little boy fell (more or less) comfortably into the groove of being back at school. Why, he even made some new friends in his class; even acquiring a "best" friend at school in one Henry Adams. Henry was a kid with a pronounced overbite needing braces, a stubborn cowlick above one eyebrow and an impish quality that seemed to endear him to teachers, parents and really... everybody. Being otherwise quite shy, the little boy would quickly learn that a person could garner certain benefits just by hanging around someone who was more popular than he and so took full advantage as his limited maturity and tentative awareness of the interaction of personalities and playground politics would allow.

Ultimately, Ricky Russell rounded out a threesome that did considerable goofing around together at school, but would only occasionally meet outside of school at Ricky's parents' home or neutral territory like the nearby, open, grassy field belonging to the Department of Water and Power and serving a dual purpose, just a stone's throw away from the little boy's home.

Smack in the middle of a parcel of land on the corner of Crebs Avenue and Collins Street opposite the little boy's home and consuming a tad more than half a neighborhood block, stood a giant steel power line tower. Other than the four steel legs of the tower bolted to cylindrical concrete piers married to earth, the rest of the area was covered in well-kept and soft green grass which was fair ground for the kids to play on and around whenever allowed outside the home. All the kids from the neighborhood found something fun to do there including touch football, baseball, dirt clod fights, tag, hide-and-go-seek, you name it; regardless the activity, all the kids in the neighborhood got along just fine. These were the days before tranquil Valley life was destroyed by the invading hordes of illegal aliens arriving from all previously untapped parts of the Third World.

There was another boy a year older living around the corner on Crebs Avenue named Nick Stewart. His family had a successful landscaping business they operated out of their home. Finding a friend in the other, Nick and the little boy would pal around together, probably playing catch or some other activity at the DWP field right across the street from Nick's house when not at school, where they seldom met.

After this coming Christmas, when Santa Claus would finally be revealed as being really his parents in fact and they bought sister E.D. and the little boy each a Huffy beach cruiser type bicycle, Nick and the little boy would always be found riding their bikes all around the neighborhood. They'd ride up to Jake's Jug for a candy bar or over to a house nearby on Tampa Ave where professional aerialists lived and had a circus quality trapeze apparatus set up in their backyard; on occasional weekends the boys would go over there just to sit on their bikes on the sidewalk out front and watch the performers practice various flying trapeze routines. Sometimes they would ride all the way over to Reseda Park to watch the ducks swim while holding a worm on a fishhook underwater in the park pond or taking turns furiously spinning each other on the galvanized steel merry-go-round in a sand pit.

His daddy usually left for work around 4:30 in the afternoon and returned by the time the children had already left for school in the morning. Except for his off days, the only time the children saw their daddy was for about an hour or so after returning home from school. Daddy was stationed out of the Hollenbeck Division and drove a patrol car on the dark and dangerous L.A. streets with a seasoned partner. His beat was right on the southwest edge of downtown Los Angeles, a very old and tired neighborhood populated nearly 100% Latino today; however, back in the day Hollenbeck Division encompassed a mostly African-American community. Let's just say the environment at work did not soften his daddy's racial intolerance, which indeed worsened over time and many an invective was made during these years as the man was incapable of not bringing his work home with him every stinking morning.

There were usually two recurring themes at the root of strife between his parents. First, were Mommy's complaints they didn't have any friends with whom they regularly socialized; and second, she further objected to the manner in which his daddy disciplined their son and the alarming regularity of its application.

Moreover, in addition to this defense of the little boy, his mommy also objected to the fact that never was sister E.D., she no particular angel, ever subject to any paternally administered corporal punishment; whereas, the little boy was never subject to anything less than corporal punishment, no matter how minor an offense in the eyes of an impartial observer. Of particular significance was Mommy's demand that Daddy stop allowing *rage* to motivate his actions when dealing with the little boy's behavior he found objectionable.

One Saturday morning months after the little boy began 3rd grade, there was a huge fight between the parents wherein Mommy put her foot down and this time would not let his daddy spank the child for the commission of some perceived infraction. As the argument progressed there was floated a suggestion that appeared to be the compromise his mommy was seeking and would be a new policy with which Daddy was going to adhere. When the eavesdropping children surmised the significance of their parent's newly adopted methodology to ensure equal justice between them, coupled with their daddy's need to temper the release of his overall rage, they each became extremely agitated and in near unison started bawling so ferociously their parents had to suspend the conflict to assuage their children's abject fear.

The suggestion immediately offered (and thankfully abandoned sometime after the children's outburst) was that, should the little boy go astray, daddy would agree to no longer punish him with any type of spanking or other corporal punishment... *at the time he so transgressed*. Neither would daddy hold sister E.D. to any form of punishment, if somehow she deserved it... *at the time of her transgression*. No! Rather... and regardless whether either child did or did **not** do <u>*anything at all*</u> to cause either parent *any* distress during the week; nevertheless, the children would be equally punished with a good (and yet equal in measure) spanking to the butt, on a designated day, once per week. *Both children* would be similarly punished; *whether either or neither* did anything to deserve any punishment at all, such an inconvenience would bear no significance in their execution of purpose.

This foolishness was what two "adults" decided was the best solution for a father, who couldn't control the anger he always harbored toward life, but instead found another outlet for his frustration on the backside of a little boy. When this particular dustup settled a few days later, there were no effective changes in the frequency of the little boy's blip on Daddy's radar, as for sister E.D. well, she continued to soar pseudo-angelic.

In fairness to his daddy, the beatings fueled by *unharnessed* rage would soon enough become a thing of the past. Nevertheless, some measure of anger always motivated the reactions by which *this* father endeavored to administer all corrective measures necessary to mold a little boy into proper manhood. "Remember son, this hurts me more than it is hurting you; and it's for your own good, too."

The solution to address Mommy's first objection being dropped for lack of creativity and the second issue of concern to her foundering marriage was resolved when Daddy took matters into his own hands to make requested changes in their social life. Late that fall and with no context explained unto the children, two strangers came into their life and became their mommy and daddy's new best friends, the enigmatic Rob and Sabina. A childless couple, they also lived on Crebs Avenue about 4 or 5 miles north in Reseda.

The kids first met the couple one Saturday after walking home from an afternoon matinee at the Corbin. The movie was West Side Story and within minutes of returning the kids were tapped to perform for the new strangers, at their mommy's urging, the "Jet Song" routine from the film. Since she'd had the phonograph album of the movie soundtrack now for weeks, the kids already knew the tune by heart and Mommy wanted them to improvise the dance number having just seen it on the big screen. Like trained monkeys, the kids amused the elders with only a vague idea what the hell they were doing and with no talent for doing it, either.

The little boy would become instantly chummy with Rob because of the beautiful machine he found parked in their driveway when returning home that day. Rob's ride was a brand-new, spankin'-hot 1963 Chevy Corvette Stingray split-window coupe and the little boy was absolutely living a dream that someone who owned such a car would now be their new family friend. Within half an hour of the lame minstrel show, Rob gave him permission to wash the car and dream became a fantastic reality. That little boy was NEVER happier in his short life as he was that afternoon for the simple privilege of being allowed to wash a stupid car; while the whole time he experienced the strangest sensation of power steeped in sexuality he recognized growing within him but couldn't usefully comprehend how to harness for himself.

The two things upon which he focused his life's attention outside of school were Major League baseball and automobiles or motorcycles. The little boy was so adept at identifying every car on the road that he could even do it at nighttime simply by identifying the patterns of light that emanated from either side of the car, front or back. Just by looking at either the headlights or the tail lights glowing in the dark he was able to tell his parents what kind of car was in front of or behind them. He was never wrong for quite a number of years until the late 60s, when Datsuns began popping up like weeds all over the Valley and he began to tire of a useless exercise.

Being his daddy's son, he too became a model making fool and was frequently gifted with a plastic Monogram or Revell hot-rod or airplane model making kit to assemble with smelly glue and adorn with unwieldy paint; all the while having very little patience to apply either correctly. Although undeserved pride was never his vice, the product of these efforts was usually substandard with a streaky application of paint and carelessly spilled glue onto areas of plastic where it shouldn't be and a poor finish the result. Still, he never fretted too much about his lack of ability or sloppy attention to detail and he always displayed his model cars shamelessly on a shelf in his bedroom and hung the airplanes from the ceiling on fishing line.

Baseball was another matter; the little boy developed such a lifelong love of the game that it became the only game (except of course his favorite... Yahtzee) he ever deemed worthy of even existing as a pastime. Most other "games" like basketball, football, soccer and similar defend the goal type team sports were viewed by him as entirely superfluous. However, baseball would be this little boy's game. The fact that his daddy's "Daddy" was also a big baseball nut and a season ticket holder to all the Angel's games would seal the deal and the little boy was hooked on baseball for life. He would relish the soothing sound of Vin Scully's distinctive voice on the radio broadcasts of spring Dodger games, which like clockwork, always signaled the onset of a much-anticipated summer break and if the Dodgers were playing .500 baseball or better, the little boy would reside for the season in a state of qualified joy.

While the nine-year-old thoroughly understood neither, yet seeing both as inexorably interconnected, he would come to find that baseball and religion could each become something of a breeding ground for schizophrenia; of which the little boy nearly succumbed due to a lack of maturity and wisdom, together with the discernment of what was becoming his own peculiar brand of self-induced lunacy.

His new aberrant behavior started out innocently and narrowly focused; however, over the next five years, a simple prayer mutated into a monstrous and thoughtless obsession. When he finally recognized the negativity for what it was, he instantly avowed to abandon the practice as rank superstition; which gave him real opportunity to rationally examine religious dogma and extract for himself the full measure of God's awesome truth and see His elegant plan.

As the influence of church doctrine melded with the superstition that enslaves many a baseball player, he somehow became convinced that his life might find more balance... or something... if he were just a little more grateful for the simple things that came his way in life. One of those things of which he should be thankful was the time he was allowed to wash Rob's '63 Stingray. Soon enough he would be in a place where another one of those bitchen cars would be found, so naturally, he *should* (and must) be grateful simply for the privilege of the vision alone.

Coming from a family that pinched every penny, there were not too many ego stimulators available for him to easily grasp, so the little boy seized vicariously upon the good fortune other people apparently experienced. From that Saturday afternoon he got to wash Rob's 'Vette forward, whenever it graced his sensory perception that he happened to view any Corvette of any model year, he would verbally (yet, under his breath) and without exception thank Jesus every time he witnessed the sight.

Once the obsessive-compulsive behavior takes a toehold, the triggers only tend to expand, never reduce. After the Corvette icon, the next automobile to become an object of his idolatry was the Jaguar XKE. When his Aunt Caro learned the little boy thought the Stingray was the finest mechanical thing ever produced, she suggested he check out the Jag. Of course, once he stumbled upon one in a parking lot somewhere, he immediately thanked the good Lord for his good fortune.

Well, it didn't stop with the Jag; and the venue of the observation expanded to include anytime one of the chosen icons were seen so much as appearing on a TV show or a in movie he happened to be watching. Of course, the obsession progressed slowly at first and was mostly restricted to cars that were rarely seen on the streets at the time. The cars desired went from the Stingray to the Jag to James Bond's Astin Martin to probably a Ferrari or Porsche, to a Harley-Davidson motorcycle, to a... well, there's no telling how it all progressed. Nevertheless, the obsession eventually spun totally out of control until the little boy became incapable of finding a vehicle with which he *could* finally draw the line.

This behavior may sound here benign, in reality it was shear lunacy until he finally put his foot down and abandoned the practice altogether by age fourteen. By that stage his obsession, absent any real sincerity, became pure superstition and his prayer nothing more than obliviously delivered rote. To his credit, once he started thanking Jesus when something as lame as a Volkswagen Squareback rolled by, he began to recognize the behavior for what it was and eventually stopped doing it altogether cold turkey.

It was not a matter of him falling into a disbelief of God or Jesus or anything like that; it was more a recognition that unrestrained religious foolishness was likely nothing more than superstition and since Jesus wanted only his *faith*, not a thoughtless engrossment of materialism, he had better knock it all off. Ever since then, the little boy and Jesus seem to have gotten along just fine with all superstition since deemed of satanic origin and hence falling forever into disrepute. An obsession fading into valuable experience from which priceless lessons melded with timely sensibility.

Since receiving "First Communion" early in his ninth year, the little boy continued only halfheartedly with his Catholic studies. However, by the time he reached that ninth birthday he was having serious doubts about how religion, and particularly Catholicism, would continue to fit into his life. It had nothing to do about questioning God's existence; more succinctly it was his ability to reconcile religion and the precepts required of leading a good Christian life, with the reality of a personal existence entirely at odds with these teachings. It wasn't a question of faith either, he had faith in abundance and always would; no, it was the rock of Christian *love* upon which he stumbled and veered.

How in hell was he ever going to conjure up any love for his neighbor... *as he loved himself*? Worse yet, he was going to have to love his *enemy*, too... not in this friggin' lifetime! Hell, he could barely tolerate the person in whose body he was temporarily occupying in this sick cosmic ballet through which he was being forced to suffer. Of course, his immaturity would allow him no significant cognizance of the subtleties of his own limited internal capacity; and, even though he really did want to be a good Christian, deep down inside his capacity to love *anybody* at all had already been permanently crippled.

There was no doubt he loved his mommy and that she loved him; however, beyond that, if his feelings for his mommy were indications of the true characteristics of that thing called love, he did not have other such feelings for any other human being. Even his daddy's "Daddy's" and Gramma Beryl's efforts to buy the little boy's affections held certain ominous implications after the gift of the satiny Roy Rogers cowboy suit turned into a violent debacle. Ignorant of his own insincerity, any expression of love ever offered either his daddy or sister E.D., or any of the other relatives associated with his family, were essentially empty words with hollow intent. His personal storehouse of love was nothing more than an empty pantry.

Even his ability to empathize on any meaningful personal level was compromised. While it's true he could express (within his own limited ability to grasp for some measure of) true feelings reflecting empathy and humanity; still, he could only do so at a safe distance. As long as there would be no chance he would have to *personally* express any feelings of either sincere condolence or feigned congratulations, he could be and would be quite empathetic to the experiences of others, particularly if a helpless animal were involved. This defense of neurotic detachment giving him results he didn't even know he was seeking; a license to never let anyone anywhere near his inner sanctum meta-morphing into a personal fortress asylum.

Confounding matters were sporadic moments when he may happen to come across a little girl whom he found particularly attractive. Of course, with no grasp of the actual components of true love, the little boy would begin a pattern of wholly mistaking base feelings of attraction as the bellwether proving everlasting love.

Unfortunately, in the mind of a mixed-up little boy, attraction was not an indication that love was possible... rather, the fact of attraction itself was THE indication love was omnipresent in the possible future relationship. Even though he still didn't quite understand how his dick fit into the whole scheme of things, he nevertheless came to believe that feelings of attraction would naturally and automatically blossom, at a minimum, into loving affection. As he matured, he erroneously relied upon the overall presumption that attraction naturally led to affection and by further extrapolation, attraction automatically presumed a thing greater than mere affection; and whatever *that thing* was, it seemed somehow to have something to do with his penis. To the pathetic, misguided lad, such was the meaning of the verb: to love.

Whether it was the love a good Christian affords his fellow man or the kind of love one achieves in a physical human relationship, the little boy had it all balled up and ass-backward. He would never become truly aware of his own confusion until it was entirely too late to correctly alter the comprehension of his mangled psyche.

There was also the matter of the bookcase in the hallway just outside of the little boy's bedroom door. It was on the bottom shelf that his daddy stored a meager collection of contemporary Playboy magazines during a time where a discovery of utter wonderment awaited a frustrated little boy seeking some measure of relief. Those magazines, viewed only when Mommy and Daddy were away from home, complemented such relief splendidly. Unfortunately, his frustration was something that always greeted him with every passing day and his primary remedy soon became an abhorrent crutch.

Even with the visual aids that, let's face it, were not nearly as revealing or graphic as those found in today's culture, the little boy was becoming persuaded that the thing he pees through must have something else to do with human existence. His first clue was revealed with how it reacted when he saw the naked Playboy girls and how warm and fuzzy that made him feel; yet, he still didn't have a clue what it was all about and he certainly wasn't in any position to ask anybody about it, either. He knew for sure there would be consequences for the asking and he didn't want to discover their extent. This stuff was way too personal to inquire of anyone else and definitely not his parents, each having clearly demonstrated their ability to unexpectedly betray his *trust,* and with a history of making him pay for that kind of foolishness.

Nevertheless, the little boy and Hugh Hefner were pals of sorts... until one day when confronted by his daddy, who made it known there was plenty of evidence suggesting the child had been pawing his way through flesh printed on the bound pages nestled peacefully on the hallway bookshelf. Under terms not ambiguous, he was to immediately cease and desist from further forays into Daddy's personal world of pornography. "Yes, Daddy; I will do whatever you say." Except he didn't, and his dumb-ass daddy never moved the offending collection out of harm's way.

His mommy's objections to Daddy's erratic behavior directed toward the little boy seemed beginning to get results. His modest existence was no longer abruptly punctuated by any extraordinary outbursts of daddy on child violence; at least, not anything the little boy hadn't already experienced and certainly nothing as drastic as those indecencies previously illustrated.

However, it wasn't a case that the nine-year-old never suffered any more corporal punishment at the hand of his daddy; it was only a case that his daddy had somehow learned how to administrate a greater measure of self-control as he administered his open palm on the buttocks of the little boy, as necessary. Excepting, the physical affect Daddy intended in the spanking had naturally diminished like the analgesic effect of callouses layered upon skin thickened through past wear and tear. Now, when his daddy would turn him over his knee to spank him the little boy just let his body, as if resigned to its fate, simply react by turning himself into dead weight and laying completely limp on the man's lap. As if acknowledging the effectiveness of this unexpected act, his daddy would finish off the spanking by resorting to ridicule, and embarrassment, and intimidation; interminably delivered.

With his daddy droning on, hurling invective intending to belittle him, the little boy began to experience a sensation as if he were physically shrinking in size so that by the time the haranguing was complete, he would feel as if his torso and legs had completely disappeared; leaving him just a head sitting on hip bone staring at his feet that seemed only about 4 inches away from his nose.

It was one of the strangest physical sensations he ever experienced in life and not one necessarily isolated to a daddy-instigated upbraiding. The anomaly would reoccur under times when great stress combined with (the stressor causing him) a prolonged period of seated immobility and silence during the hectoring. Adults have reported similar out of body experiences at certain times, such as when getting vocally reamed at work in the boss's office and having to sit there silently absorbing interminable admonishment.

Once school dismissed for the summer break of 1963, there was a reinvigoration of the relationship between the little boy's mommy and daddy that took an interesting twist in Mommy's after work activities, two days a week for about eight weeks. In a misguided effort to find more common ground, his daddy persuaded Mommy to take up SCUBA diving; you know, so they could do stuff together! Never mind that this activity is very intense and consumes a whole lot of time in which to safely participate. Never mind about what exactly the children (who, in all practicality could not be included as active players) were going to do while the parents were bobbing up and down out on the ocean. The adults were simply not thinking clearly. Nevertheless, his mommy joined the Rocketdyne company SCUBA diving club that June and began taking lessons offered as a company perk after work.

The biweekly trips to the Rocketdyne recreation center located at Roscoe Boulevard and Fallbrook Avenue were a blast for the little boy. While Mommy was at SCUBA classes, he and sister E.D. had use of a playground where they made friends with children of other diving school students. The kids would compete on the big swing set against each other to see who could fly the farthest away after hurling themselves off the saddle as the pendulum reached the end of its ascension and landing 10 or 15 feet away in the big sand pit occupied also by a merry-go-round, jungle gym and slide; all steel and all galvanized to prevent their rusting.

Given free rein, the kids were left unattended to fool around all over this huge compound intended mostly for adults, yet with enough kid friendly attractions just perfect for a curious kid to waste some time while Mommy wondered what the hell she had gotten herself into. Although his mommy soldiered on admirably and completely, her experience during those sixteen days, late that spring, couldn't have been nearly as much fun as were the little boy's and probably sister E.D.'s, too.

All diver certification class protocols require several practical, in the water lessons in a swimming pool. After proficiency is demonstrated in the pool, some kind of an ocean (or lake) "check-out" dive is required; often both a shallow water (or beach) dive *and* a deep-water dive (via a boat) in the ocean or a lake, where the instructor scrutinizes student proficiency, adherence to safety protocol and the like. In his mommy's case, it was determined that she would make her check-out dive during a Rocketdyne company dive club trip to Monterey, California on the coming Independence Day; for which the family would take a long weekend. They would make it a camping event and his daddy tapped Uncle Gus once again for the use of his camper and truck.

The adults would do their SCUBA thing in a big cove near their campground on the Saturday after the holiday and on Sunday the whole family would see what was so special about Monterrey; of which town the little boy was decidedly unimpressed. Maybe today with that bitchen new aquarium Monterrey might be a bit more attractive to him; however, the family's side trip into town was exceptionally boring for the little boy.

Especially boring since earlier that very morning, after waking in the tent he shared with sister E.D. while their parents slept in Gus's camper, the little boy was for once treated by his daddy just like a little man who'd finally earned the old man's trust. After the family ate their breakfast, the little boy's daddy took him on a walk up a dirt trail away from the campground and over by some beachside bluffs. Once at their destination his daddy taught the little boy how to shoot his 6" Smith policeman's service revolver at tin cans they brought along for targets. Now *that* was fun and for a nine-year-old rookie he demonstrated a pretty good aim indeed. Not once did the thought of turning that gun on his father ever occur to him, either. Go figure.

There would be one problem of the little boy's own making cropping up very soon after the return from Monterrey and what was his mommy's successful check-out dive and subsequently awarded Los Angeles County diver's certification.

This time the trouble all began with a prank gift given to his mommy by her boss in recognition of receiving her diver's certificate and combined with the fact that the prank was an ersatz award suitably framed that included a (non-nude, yet still ribald) John Dempsey cartoon featuring two SCUBA divers that was published in a recent Playboy magazine; the magazine the little boy had already been warned by his daddy he must avoid. Displayed upon the cartoon portion of the award was a personalized thought balloon making some cutesy reference to Mommy's recent achievement.

Although always reticent around the adults in his life for better or worse, the little boy was sharp as a tack with an outstanding memory. Unfortunately, he vividly remembered that cartoon from *somewhere*, and although he could not quite remember *where*, he was filled with certainty its source would come back to him eventually. A fact he was proud to boisterously announce to all and sundry listening.

The hilarious part was, as he strutted all around telling the adults he was certain he had seen that cartoon somewhere before and the adults, all knowing its source, just let him continue digging that hole for a good long while. Before too long and with dramatic effect his daddy showed the little boy that the very cartoon on Mommy's trophy could also be found that moment on the very same page directly behind Miss April's fine round ass located on Daddy's bookshelf in the hall. The revelation caused him to feel as if suddenly shrinking with nothing remaining but a head resting wobbly on his hips and eyes staring at tippy-toes just inches away; his torso and legs metaphysically ripped from him under the sufferance of abject embarrassment.

Within two months of the beginning of the school year, exactly 52 days after his ninth birthday celebration, the nation would lose a President to assassination. At about 11:45 that Friday morning, the little boy's teacher suddenly left the classroom only to return shortly with tear-filled eyes and to give the class a solemn, sniffling notification of the tragedy. The class (indeed, the whole school) was dismissed and all the kids sent home where, for the rest of the day, the little boy watched non-stop TV coverage of breaking events in the investigation of who-dun-it.

When the siblings walked in the front door together, they

found their father, clad only in his bleached white "skivvies" (Navy slang for Daddy's boxer shorts) and standing at an ironing board pressing his police uniform trousers flat before leaving for work later that afternoon. However, this vision, coupled with the horrible events of the day put the scenario they witnessed into the realm of the absurd and the little boy had tremendous difficulty grasping at something that seemed so surreal and unnatural at a time he was under the distinct impression he should be otherwise filled with fear and sadness.

Immediately peculiar was the appearance that Daddy seemed totally unaware of what had just occurred and at the same time not surprised to see the kids home early from school. What the little boy next ascertained was that his daddy was indeed aware of the nation's loss; hell, he was watching the damn thing on TV at that very moment. The fact of the matter was that his daddy simply didn't care at all that this tragic event had happened; NOT ONE BIT.

The manner in which his daddy displayed this odd brand of callousness began for the little boy an entire weekend most bizarre; indeed, immediately upon waking that Sunday morning he watched Jack Ruby shoot Oswald in the gut and kill him on a live TV broadcast preempting the Sunday gospel shows. Since his daddy was sleeping off the night shift, the little boy would never learn whether his daddy approved of this particular murder or not; however, some guy blowin' that fuckin' Kennedy's brains out... ooo-rah. Of that fact, the little boy would have no doubt.

The clash between his mommy, crushed by events and his daddy's shameless ambivalence that a man he didn't like (much less the President of their nation) was just viciously murdered demonstrated more craziness than the little boy was willing to take. For relief, he would be forced to make more than one trip to the bathroom that weekend, where he could rub furiously what the other boys at school told him was called a boner. He wouldn't become any less confused once relieved, only less frustrated that there was nothing immediate he could do to remove himself from vexing and bitter circumstances.

There was a cold wind blowing in that home the rest of the afternoon before his daddy left for work and all of it was from tension between parents who couldn't be more incompatible with one another. While the kids, isolated from the battle were left to either grieve or rejoice; and with his daddy's obvious and vitriolic disdain, the little boy was far from certain which direction was the correct course for him to take. The only track record he had before him in which to rely upon allowed that he'd best never let his daddy find out he held a view that might somehow come into Daddy's disfavor. Suffice to say that Monday and a new school day would come along none too soon as the only avenue to escape the madness possessed of at least one of the adults living in this home.

Chapter 6

*A*n unexpected surprise ushered in the summer of 1964 precipitating some unwelcomed experiences. Both children would spend a full week away from their home and parents and alternatively would be vacationing at the Lazy J Ranch Camp, beginning the second week after school let out for summer break. They would be dropped off at the camp on Friday afternoon and wouldn't be retrieved until early afternoon, seven days from Saturday.

Right off the bat, the little boy managed to alienate everybody from the counselors on down before sunset the evening of his first full day at camp. Coming as a shock to the nine-year-old was bitter realization that all the Lazy J campers were already rabid environmentalists years before anyone ever heard of "ecology" or experienced the fanatics this new anti-capitalist movement would spawn. Typical for everything he would ever do that carried with it great significance, the little boy would herein learn a hard lesson of his fellow camper's sensitivities, except only doing so after murderously violating them.

The Lazy J had it all: a big-ass swimming pool; horseback riding among rolling, straw-covered hills; archery; arts and crafts; evening bonfires with sing-a-longs and ghost stories. The whole shebang a camper's Valhalla. Located about a mile west of the intersection at Valley Circle (where the road continuing west became a private, unimproved road) on Roscoe Boulevard.

Although he might have otherwise been looking forward to

the quintessential sleep-away experience, the little boy was entirely ill suited to this adventure under the circumstances of his prior upbringing and present level of social maturity. Irrespective of the indiscretion coming to his immediate future, the little boy in this setting became a natural outcast the moment he entered the property. However, he didn't know of the fact until he demonstrated it before the camp's entire populace and thereafter experienced the universally negative result of his actions. Within 30 hours of embarking on a normal child's rite of passage he became the camp pariah and shunned by all excepting perhaps sister E.D., for the rest of a long-ass, miserable week.

His night of personal infamy came on the evening of that first Saturday after supper. To say it came as a shock isn't properly descriptive of the emotions the little boy experienced. In his heart of hearts, he truly believed he was selflessly performing Herculean service for the entire establishment... And, what about the children? Shit, he was saving the fucking *DAY*; except, none of those other little bastards appreciated the effort... NO. Indeed, all and sundry, from children and staff to the fireflies and ants, were quite appalled and not at all by the formidable threat extinguished through the bravery of one little boy.

The incident occurred as all the children were gathered in front of an outdoor stage of sorts and seated on the grassy meadow between it and an enormous, very old oak tree about 20 yards away from the stage. The event was part entertaining pep rally, part welcome to the camp type orientation gathering for the week's new campers. There was a circular patch of thick, dark green ivy about 30 feet in diameter that surrounded the oak, with occasional ivy vines creeping up the tree's thick trunk awaiting the trimming necessary to prevent their eventually suffocating the ancient thing.

Apparently, the festivities presented on stage were not too interesting and the little boy, sitting at the back of the crowd, very near the edge where ivy met grass and nursing an orange soda had his fascination otherwise distracted by something else a few feet away. He saw two little girls gawking and pointing at something of which the little boy immediately jumped up to investigate. The girls had discovered a giant, hairy, jet-black tarantula spider wandering away from the safety of the ivy patch and creeping silently toward the children seated on the grass, between the scary creature and the stage.

Perhaps his indoctrination as Smokey the safety boy may take a share of the blame because it was always his intention to keep everyone safe and nothing more. Nonetheless for his part, this was going to be an opportunity upon which he would sacrifice his safety for everybody present and hopefully emerge the camp's *hero*.

That he was motivated by a longing for some measure of recognition as a human being is revealed clearly by the fact that before boldly acting to secure the area, he yelled loud enough for everybody assembled to hear, "Tarantula" and then promptly squashed that hideous beast flat, between the sole of his Jack Purcell sneaker and 3-inch blades of soft green grass. Instead of the hero's reception he presumed obvious after such a brave execution of necessary monster control, his personal universe suddenly and unexpectedly crashed into a cacophony of rather caustic outrage directed his way.

It seems the offending arachnid was in fact a critter that enjoyed widespread affection among many of the other campers and was but a tidbit of a dynamic that occurs at a place like the Lazy J Ranch; of which the little boy was clueless. He and sister E.D. were first timers here and short timers, too. Many of the other kids attending camp were veteran campers and probably knew more about the place than did some of the camp's counselors. Alas, the appearance of this fuzzy black creature was not something unexpected by the regulars; but he was way too quick to act and in so doing murdered the camp's mini mascot Terrence, just as the last rays of sunshine evaporated behind the hilltops surrounding them.

The rest of the week was uneventful as the little boy was now keeping very much to himself, yet still participating in all the scheduled activities offered by the daily curriculum. Sister E.D.'s presence at the camp was essentially unaffected by her association with the heinous little boy and she readily made friends with other little girls who didn't blame her for her brother's crime; therefore, he was left alone the rest of the week to amuse himself by way of his own devices.

All children attending camp were each allowed a maximum 50-cent daily budget to spend after each day's activities, which the camp authorities doled out daily per all the parent's pre-authorized instruction. The general practice was usually 25 cents for a soda every night and the remainder for perhaps an ice cream sandwich or candy bar, maybe a few other choices. The little boy would only spend half of his budget on himself, buying an orange soda every evening and saving the other 25 cents for later. On one occasion even spending some money saved for a postcard to send home to his mommy; for the 1964 perspective, we're talking a 7-cent postcard and a 3-cent stamp.

He would learn of a special event at the end of the week where a day trip was planned to a rich kid's camp affiliated with the Lazy J, high in the Santa Monica Mountains and overlooking the Pacific Ocean; the spending allotment that day was a whole dollar, but his parents only had funds enough for a budget of 50-cents for each of their two kids. He would need some extra money for that day trip and saving some of his daily allowance in anticipation of it seemed to him perfectly sensible. The occasion was going to be a swimming competition between the destination camp and any plucky Lazy J camper with a tendency to use feet as flippers. This was an event straight up the little boy's alley and he fearlessly signed on as competitor.

On the morning of the trip to the rich kid's camp, all the Lazy J kids were transported there (and returned) in the back of a 5-ton stake-bed truck; with nobody but the driver and two other counselors riding in the cab up front and the only beings in the vehicle with a proper seat upon which to sit. The big truck was a general-purpose machine the Lazy J used for everything from affecting hay deliveries to the camp's livestock barn, to shlepping a gaggle of kids around town. For this trip they would utilize the bed of the truck, probably 18 or 20 feet long, which was packed wall-to-wall with a cluster of children seated on nothing more than a slab of work-worn sheet steel.

Sure, there were wooden slat panels all around the edge of the truck's bed high enough to keep everybody onboard... however, if there was a crash, there definitely would have been a mass of ugly carnage. Hell, if they pulled that kind of crap today and were pulled over by the cops with all those kids exposed like that, the driver would be jailed immediately and the owner of the camp would be in for a real shitstorm. Believe it or not, these were the good old days when everybody minded his or her own friggin business.

The excursion took them east on Roscoe to Topanga Canyon Boulevard, through the Valley south, over the hill and through Topanga Canyon and the Santa Monica Mountains to the Pacific Coast Highway. From PCH, they turned north and continued past Malibu and the world famous Surfrider Beach, until somewhere around Corral Canyon where they turned again inland and continued up into the Santa Monica Mountains to the "camp" about 3 miles from the coast and about 3,500 feet in elevation.

Compared to the ramshackle plywood cabins resting upon the omnipresent dirt and dust that gave the Lazy J its charm, the rich kid's facility was NOT, by that definition, a "camp". The Lazy J did not have brick and mortar bunkhouses; nor lush, professional landscaping and concrete pathways leading to a first-class recreation center, an Olympic swimming pool with the full complement of similar quality diving apparatus. It was much more resort than a camp and was definitely built and maintained for folks the little boy knew had more disposable resources than his family ever would.

Winning a Blue Ribbon each for the 100-meter freestyle *and* (the first leg of) the 400-meter relay team, the swimming competition for the little boy was for him a mini-triumph. The competitive activities were all wrapped up by about 3 o'clock, whereupon the Lazy J campers piled onto the bed of the 5-ton truck and motored down the mountain and back to the coast highway.

About a mile or two after passing by the Malibu Pier, the truck pulled over at the Frosty Freeze located on the PCH for many, many... many years. There, the little boy's patience in saving the past week's allowance finally paid off, as he could now buy the largest frosty cone they sold, *and*... he could have the thing dipped in that yummy liquid chocolate coating that turned solid and crunchy after coming out of the dipping vat. Once he finished that 50-cent frosty cone, he had just enough money left to buy yet another; this time selecting banana flavored ice cream and paying extra for a double chocolate dipping.

It was a mistake to make this stop for ice cream for two reasons, from the perspective of the children riding in the back of the truck in one instance, and from the little boy's personal perspective, in the other. The first incident of error came just as the truck crested the hill upon which Topanga Canyon Boulevard begins its descent back into the Valley. As the downhill speed increased gradually and the curves in the road became a little more aggressive, the little stomachs began churning from an over indulgence of frosty deliciousness until nature finally took its course among more than one of the intrepid riders.

Suddenly, a pool of vomit at least six feet in diameter appeared in the middle of the seating area of those kids and immediately created an odd antimagnetic repulsion among them all. It was quite amusing to the little boy who observed upon their early morning departure that one more child couldn't possibly be crammed onto the back of that truck; however, once the contents of delicate bellies began hurling, there magically appeared all kind of extra seating room.

By the time they returned to the Lazy J, the little boy himself was fighting off stomach cramps and the urge to crap in the swimming trunks he was wearing underneath his jeans. Just as time for public humiliation was nigh upon him, the big 5-ton flatbed truck pulled onto the compound and the little boy could see much needed relief, in the privacy of the john attached to his living quarters, happily happening in his immediate future.

The plywood cabin he shared with about 15 or 20 other boys accommodated everybody bunking therein with a one-toilet bathroom installed in a corner of the building. All during the week there was a fat little bastard with a bunk sharing the little boy's cabin who thought it was hilarious to burst in on other unsuspecting boys and harass them while they were trying to take a dump. Bully-boy repeated this rudeness simply to embarrass the kids and although the little boy had yet to be similarly victimized, he had already vowed to himself if this fat-bodied prick played this prank on him, there would be a fat price to pay for the doing.

It was upon running into the john immediately after jumping off the flatbed truck when the little porker decided it was the little boy's turn for his peculiar brand of humor. Now, it wasn't a matter that he was expecting the assault; it was more a matter of the urgency of his business facilitating rapid completion of the task. At once the troublemaker burst into the bathroom and the little boy was no longer distracted, having pulled up his swimsuit and just starting to button his 501 Levi's, he stood ready to affect the immediate repulse of fat boy's intrusion.

The two boys came flying out of the head, ran through the cabin and out onto a big open area between their cabin and then the others, through which they each sprinted. The fat boy was deceptively quick and managed to escape the little boy's clutches as he darted underneath one of the girl's cabins a few hundred feet away from where the ballyhoo all began. Given the fact the little boy's claustrophobia had already been fully cemented on the day his satiny Roy Rogers cowboy suit was torn to bits, there was no way in hell he was going to follow that kid any farther underneath that building.

It was indeed a good thing the dustup ended as simply as it did since the little boy didn't have a clue how to fight anybody in any fashion; never having done it nor having been taught anything by his daddy about fist fighting, boxing, or anything of the sort. In reality, since the other boy ran for cover, the little boy considered himself the clear victor even though he never landed a single blow upon his opponent.

If other boy had merely stood his ground, there might have been a very different outcome; since he didn't, the little boy learned early on that intimidation was a very powerful thing, *if applied effectively*. About a year and a half later he would learn, again the hard way, that intimidation as a defense mechanism has its limitations and without a repertoire of offensive techniques backing it up, he would suffer several ass-kicking's at the hands of other boys in his school.

The week at camp met its end the next day at around 1:00 o'clock when their daddy came to retrieve the little boy and E.D., his little sister. His excitement was solely reserved in anticipation of seeing his mommy; except, it was Daddy alone in his '62 Monza with no mommy in sight. Immediately upon greeting the children, a deception began and remained hidden until revealed as subterfuge in the coming weeks. Despite his daddy's claim, there seemed to the little boy something else quite amiss beyond the events immediately relayed unto the children. As the matter unfolded over the next week or so, he was presented evidence entirely incongruous with the excuse given as justification for the reason they're not returning immediately home after the week at the Lazy J Ranch Camp.

Something was up, but he just couldn't put his finger on exactly what the fuck was going on between these two adults, his nutty parents. Of course, the little boy at this time held no ability to discern normal from abnormal behavior when it came to familial relations; however, that didn't mean he was incapable of observing obvious inconsistencies between words and actions and how each cooperated with his own visual experience. Although still just a young boy, he would feel an emotional response (he later identified as insult) anytime his parents pulled this kind of crap.

Since the day the little boy was blessed with the opportunity to wash Rob's (of Rob and Sabina fame) Corvette Stingray, the mysterious couple were seldom seen and never spoken of within his earshot. When he did on occasion see him and ask Rob about the Stingray, the answers were always nebulous. Although the puzzle sorted itself out piecemeal, ultimately, he was able to discern the fact that Rob was a car salesman and in reality, his daddy's buddy at the Chevy dealership nearby the police academy where he bought the Monza. It also turned out the Stingray belonged to the dealership and Rob had borrowed it on the occasion of their first visit.

Now suddenly, Rob and Sabina re-entered their lives in a big way and the negative influence they contributed, soon to directly affect the kids, would for just a while longer remain to the little boy another mystery to be sorted through.

It all began during the week the children were doing their sleepover at the Lazy J Ranch Camp when Mommy traded in her 1956 Renault Dauphine death trap for a 1955 Buick Special Coupe, a 3,500-pound land-yacht with two big chrome titties jutting out from the front bumper. As it turned out, good-old Rob was the salesman brokering this deal, too.

"Now, I want you to know she's gonna be perfectly okay and I don't want you kids to get scared, but your mommy was in a bad car accident and will have to spend the next week or so in the hospital," Daddy informed the little boy and sister E.D. in lieu of another kind of greeting after a long week apart.

This was apparently a complete lie, except the aspect of Mommy being okay. Ultimately it would be revealed his mommy was shackin' up with Rob for the coming week; and Daddy would be pounding his prick into either Sabina or some other sleazo, also at this time. He probably was defiling the family's Tarzana home with his adultery, while Mommy was staying in Reseda on Crebs Avenue doing with Rob in private what she later couldn't help but do in front of her own two children. Meanwhile, the children would be relocated to relatives for the duration of the debauchery.

Mommy, the children were told, was in a hair-raising, single-car collision and suffered a broken collarbone. Because of her hospitalization and Daddy's work schedule, the children would be separated for the next week, where the little boy would be spending the time with Gramma Beryl and his daddy's "Daddy", while sister E.D. would stay with the widow Gramma Frances.

Although a shocking revelation and a fear filled disappointment, this was the better of the two possible arrangements since there had always been friction between the little boy and Gramma Frances. The first real indication that a car accident was not the entire story was the way in which Gramma Beryl spoiled him rotten for the next 7 or 8 days spent in their Santa Ana house; and yet any talk of Mommy in the hospital was instantly diverted, as was the notion of calling her there by telephone to find out how she was doing.

Every day started out with a hot breakfast made for him and ready on her homey kitchen table when he awoke and every day brought an exciting new activity for which he and Gramma would be mostly involved together while "Grampa" was at work. One evening they went to the county fair and "Grampa" came along with them. The place was a scramble of human activity, flashing lights and extraordinary noises; the little boy even got to watch a man being shot out of a cannon and flying into a net 200 feet away.

He and Gramma went to the beach one day where the little boy hunted for sand crabs after tiring from doing as much body surfing as he possibly could. On another day they visited a family Gramma said was her sister's, a woman married to a farmer in El Toro where the little boy got to fly a kite farther than he ever did before; until misfortune caused it to lose its lift and crash into the family's corn field (in what seemed) a mile away by the time it was retrieved by he and his cousin. He became fascinated by the family's tractor and after being given a ride atop the thing; he developed an odd, lifelong nostalgia for all manner of those magnificent machines.

Naturally, every evening was capped with the opportunity to watch TV *in color*; sister E.D. wasn't watching no stinking color TV, that's for sure. Let us not forget the ever-popular Yahtzee games that were a house favorite and played with boisterous regularity. The evenings spent with the paternal Gram's this week would hold for him a special allure; when they would jiggle those five dice in their own shaker cups at the kitchen table, the little boy would actually begin to feel like he fit right into the situation, a real being acting like a real grown-up.

Aside from the fact the rattletrap Renault was gone and replaced with the big Buick when returning home a week later, other indications there was no life-threatening car accident were the absence of any apparent injuries his mommy should have suffered had there indeed been the harrowing crash described.

Indeed, Mommy's car was supposed to have had its brakes lock up in a panic-stop on the Ventura Freeway, causing loss of control with the vehicle shooting across four lanes of traffic and into the chain link fence used in the 1960s as the center highway divider. Despite hitting the fence so hard it reportedly caused the car to launch up and over the fence while landing in the first lane of opposing traffic, there were no cuts or bruises visible to Mommy's hands, arms, or face and the collar bone was completely healed upon the return home; all of which the adults chalked up entirely to the week's hospital stay. The little boy knew he was born at night, but it wasn't that past night; still, who was he to argue with these knuckleheads?

One day, in a rare moment of candor with his daddy, the little boy told him of the incident at the Lazy J where he almost got into a fist fight with the fat boy but he didn't have a clue what to do had fists actually started flyin'. Of course, his daddy said he was happy to oblige but the lesson was a lame explanation of the basics and he seemed loath to demonstrate any effective technique either offensive or defensive.

A few days later, while he was mindlessly playing by himself in the front yard and his mommy and Daddy were sitting at the dining table adjacent to the picture windows that overlooked the yard, another boy unknown to the family wandered by and lingered just long enough at their yard for his daddy to coax his son into a fight with the stranger. Since the poor kid was essentially blindsided by a tackle initiated by the little boy, he was hurt and started crying immediately before running home to summon his parents for intervention.

The mess stirred up by his daddy with the other boy's daddy was Daddy's problem; the little boy's problem was the immediate guilt he felt for harming another human being without any just cause. Thereafter, and with few exceptions, he would eschew all resort to fisticuffs. However, later in life he learned the fine art of demonstrating a willingness to go to the mat, without ever intending upon doing any such thing, and using that specter to intimidate those he deemed a threat to anything to which his sensibilities objected. Almost always the technique worked very well.

On separate occasions during his first nine years of age, the little boy became afflicted with the usual childhood diseases: mumps, chicken pox and the measles. As result, he missed a week or so of school recuperating from each infection. Also, by age nine, and although sister E.D. was the only family member privy to the fact, the little boy had become infected with quite the garbage mouth and yet his parents would seemingly never be the wiser. Although not yet versed in every obscenity in the book but most, he selectively applied their salt to his speech as well any sailor strutting around a Navy submarine.

Of course, the little boy was able to practice his skill with relative impunity most of that summer at the odious Northridge day camp. Sister E.D. and the little boy were incarcerated against their will 4 hours a day, 5 days a week and forced to "interact" with a gang of savages and rank hooligans occupying the facility and acting as the enforcers of discipline; apparently doing so at the behest of camp management. Of course, he also attended his regular Cub Scout meetings once per week.

The next two years would be relatively uneventful for the little boy if you exclude: him thinking he might be falling in love and within half a year resolving silently to never fall in love again; watching his pal Nick Stewart being run over by a car right before his eyes; catching his mommy fucking Rob in their Collins Street bathroom while the children sat in the old Buick parked at the curb, unaware (for a while) of the immorality occurring inside their house. Oh... and Mommy and Daddy announcing their divorce and the little boy reacting by contracting a nasty case of impetigo and dancing at death's door from an allergic reaction to the penicillin given him to quell a hideous, puss-seeping infection to both knees and both elbows.

The brief epoch concluded with the fractured family moving into a new neighborhood where two other boys at his school learned he wouldn't fight back when picked on; thereafter making him their personal human bop bag for most of the first friggin' semester of his 5th grade. Other than that... the little boy's existence was perfectly normal and completely drama free.

Maybe it was a perfect alignment of the stars or something; regardless of reason, the little boy navigated all of July floating briefly upon a sea of personal tranquility. August however, found him floundering directionless in a flood of absolute chaos. The altercation, it turned out, would be the last firefight of the war between them and although the bullets stopped flying here, future hostilities would twist into a sick battle to win the hearts and minds of their emotionally malleable and somewhat unstable children.

It would be rare the cause of their marital strife, of which the little boy ever became aware, that had nothing at all to do with something *he* did. Indeed, never before this day had the secrets underlying the fundamental flaw to their union ever been revealed to the extent they boiled up from below the surface and spilled out all over the living room floor. Neither child knew what to do while their parents vented nearly ten years of hostility upon one another; the little boy became especially flummoxed once they began to struggle over a set of car keys and his mommy demanded he enter the fray to retrieve them from her and then bolt to keep them away from his daddy.

There was no question in his young mind with whom to take sides; it was his mommy who always defended him and now it was his turn to defend her. Not sure how to handle the matter, his reaction was pure instinct. Unable to get anywhere near the four flailing arms struggling with precious bits of jangling steel and brass, the little boy lunged for and grabbed his daddy's left leg just above the knee with both his arms, bear hug fashion, and sunk his perfectly formed numbers eight and nine incisors deep into his quadriceps.

Remarkably, his daddy did nothing, per sé, to punish the little boy for his assault. This is not to suggest he didn't react quite violently when bitten; he did. In a quite natural human response, Daddy let go of Mommy's arm holding the keys, bringing his right backhand down onto the little boy's right cheek with a thud so jarring he immediately released a mouthful of his daddy's skin and trousers.

With that coda, a cease-fire was called between all the parties and the little boy was sent outside that warm summer evening to sit on the porch and contemplate his worth in life. Mommy put sister E.D. to bed and afterward she and his daddy argued late into the night while the little boy, sitting on their front porch, couldn't shrink himself small enough to escape all the embarrassment streaming out the house and challenging the neighbors to mind their own business.

Sitting under the gloomy glow of the yellow "bug lamp" illuminating the tears coursing down his cheeks, the little boy vowed that night to never allow himself to get married, not ever. Nearly swamped by the shitstorm just witnessed, he was reduced to a trembling basket case unflinchingly persuaded marriage was a defective institution; so fatally flawed, his guts were telling him, he could never possibly live long enough to discover the ins and outs of all its complicated strictures. The rules that govern compatibility and compromise were hard enough putting into practice at school or when dealing with his pesky little sister; but when you also throw a nose-biting little bastard like him into the mix... well, this sorry incident sealed in him a lifelong determination to never put himself into a position as vulnerable as both his parents had done for themselves.

Unfortunately, his calculus ciphered under dim porch light amounted to nothing more substantial than a child's lame cost/benefit analysis, fatally flawed and hopelessly incomplete. The prospect he would never find future happiness in a relationship naively extended to his parallel and passive acceptance that the breach would also include a lifetime naturally devoid of offspring. Rejecting the implementation of reason, he mistakenly allowed momentary, yet bitter pain to obliterate any optimism he would ever find love and happiness truly satisfying components in his miserable life. Of course, had he been aware at the time about the joys of a wet vagina, perhaps the intractability of his inward pledge would soften with the stiffening of his eternally outward-facing penis.

A week or two later, the family was invited over to Rob and Sabina's house in Reseda for what was only of concern to the adults; the kids were not participants in any particular activity that may justify exactly why they shouldn't have been left at home to instead watch the Saturday afternoon "Million Dollar Movie" on Channel 9.

Once at their place, the little boy witnessed the strangest thing; Rob's hair had turned pure white since he last saw the guy.

The fact the color changed was not alone unusual, it was the excuse that was odd; even more peculiar were all the adults confirming his story as a truthful event. Supposedly, Sabina inadvertently startled him one day and unexpectedly caused his hair to turn *instantly* white from fright.

"Whatever..." he thought, and with that the little boy knew from the get-go this assertion was nothing but bullshit flying through fan-blades, which all too soon rained out any remaining summer fun and frolic with a drizzling stench.

Something else was amiss. Ordinarily the family would have relied on his daddy's Monza as conveyance for a trip such as this; instead, they took the big Buick and Mommy drove instead. The little boy's mommy never drove the car unless Daddy wasn't present and if he *was* there, his daddy *always* drove. But, not on this occasion and it was a *very* peculiar circumstance.

Not long after the colloquy regarding Rob's porn star hairdo, the kids were ordered to leave the couple's house and wait for their parents out in the Buick. Except, when she returned his mommy was accompanied not by his daddy but instead Rob was strolling out to the car with her. His mommy drove away from their house leaving his daddy behind and instead filling the front passenger seat with a guy who'd probably make Lyndon Johnson seem saintly.

Very soon after departure it was determined that Mommy had to return to Collins Street to retrieve something of nebulously suspicious necessity. Upon arriving home, his mommy ordered the children to stay in the car parked at the curb while the adults went inside to get whatever it was Mommy wanted. Unfortunately, Mommy couldn't find what it was she was searching the house for and left the kids in the car a tad-bit too long. There was considerable discussion between the little boy and sister E.D. about a proposal to disobey his mommy and enter the house to discover the cause of the delay. Since it was the little boy urging inspection, yet not disclosing his suspicion of possible malfeasance, E.D.

declined to participate but agreed the adults certainly should have by then returned.

Of course, after entering he roamed the house silently for a bit and didn't immediately see anybody. He walked down the hall past the bathroom door, which was closed, past his room and sister E.D.'s room to the master bedroom and not seeing her, called out for his mommy. There was a muffled reply coming from the bathroom door behind him, where he went to inquire what was taking Mommy so much time and that they were getting really tired of waiting outside in the car. They were at their own house, for crying out loud. His mommy assured him that everything was okay and to go back out to the car where she would return shortly. That was that. He knew from the bottom of his heart that some real shit was going on... but he didn't know what the fuck it was. Literally.

About five minutes after his inquiry the adults emerged, hopped into the car without explanation and they all drove away. After 30 or 40 minutes of driving aimlessly around Encino, Winnetka, and back to Reseda, they arrived in the driveway at Rob's house having accomplished nothing and with no apparent reason for leaving in the first place. Instructed again to wait in the Buick where, very soon, their parents rejoined and returned to the car, entered without ceremony and drove off never explaining a thing to their children.

Upon returning from his search for Mommy in the house, the little boy did indeed report to sister E.D. his observation. However, he had absolutely no idea that the object of Mommy's search was for a hot dick not belonging to his daddy. Although he'd been uttering the word fuck almost daily for three years, he still had no understanding of what the word meant; indeed, a cock to him was a rooster and a blowjob was something done to birthday cakes. Naturally, when he finally did get the memo that males and females did what they do and it was a normal and quite popular human activity, this whole incident returned to mind and the context of the experience finally crystalized into reality, away from his initial disbelief, and transformed into the reluctant acceptance of unpleasant facts.

His mommy would *never, ever, ever,* **do** something like THAT; Ichk..., would she? Wait, what the hell was going on in their bathroom that Saturday afternoon between Mommy and that creepy Rob dude? Unfortunately, once he fully accepted that humans did this activity called sex, with his very existence being proof positive Mommy herself had indeed done the nasty, such was the day her halo dimmed a little in the eyes of the little boy. Since Daddy's trespass with Sabina (or, whomever?) was without the eyewitness confirmation of his mommy's encounter with Rob, the little boy never assigned Daddy any guilt in this matter until analysis was undertaken much later.

Normally his daddy had Wednesday's off work but when he wasn't present for dinner that evening Mommy explained he was late from running errands and would be home shortly. When he did arrive there was no dinner waiting for him and the parents went immediately into a private huddle. After a few moments, they each sort of adjusted themselves as if to buck up for a task requiring their best comportment.

The little boy was by now familiar with parental separation as a temporary state of affairs and tonight he would learn of the finality of this thing called divorce, an abstraction previously unknown and totally unfathomable to him. He was far from certain how he should feel about this revelation delivered by his parents with such a matter of fact-ness he was left with no doubt about the permanence of their resolve.

Both children began to cry and to wish it wasn't true and the parents understood their fear and the uncertain impact this decision would have upon their future. The little boy remembered well the level of poverty they had just arisen out of and he was convinced this news presaged their return to less than desirable living conditions. For now, the children were assured, nothing would change; they would still be living on Collins Street and would still attend school at Tarzana Elementary. Alternatively, Daddy would be living in Wilmington and had already moved all his personal belongings to an apartment on the fringe of the L.A. Harbor. And, he would be leaving the home, permanently, that very moment.

After the children calmed down, their daddy left the house and would never again spend another night with their mommy, alone or otherwise. Almost from the moment the front door closed behind him, the propaganda battle to steal the hearts and minds of the children began in earnest and Mommy was the commanding general on the side of the angels, according to her view of things.

In all fairness to his mommy, it was his daddy who threw down the gauntlet and set the table for the only defense at her ready disposal... fear. To state now what was unknown then, the little boy's daddy not only avowed to gain full custody of her children, that vow included the taunt that the children themselves would beg Mommy (and petition the court) to be allowed to move away from her to live permanently with Daddy. It may have all been nonsense sputtered by a bitter man lost, but the little boy's young mommy considered the threat a vile personal attack.

This completely unexpected turn of events resulted in one significant consequence bolstering a shaky esteem and causing him to find an immediate remedy to what was now his vexing dilemma. The solution he adopted unwittingly allowed the little boy comforting justification to shrug off the loss of his father through a convenient distraction and the redirection of his boundless energy.

The little boy commenced a lifelong fascination for the collection of self-defense weapons of all types.

Ever since that evening the little boy stumbled upon the vagrant sleeping in the backseat of the brand new Monza he was eternally tormented by conflicted feelings between always fearing Daddy's presence versus the continual fear of some unspecified criminal incursion occurring in Daddy's absence. Once notified of the divorce, he reacted with a mixture of relief knowing he would never again be arbitrarily subjected *in this household* to nonsensical outbursts of paternal rage and with concurrent trepidation in the certain knowledge he was now the man of the house and by extension now charged with responsibility for all family security.

With Daddy no longer the center of the little boy's emotional universe, he was free to discard most daddy centered fear and able to now concentrate all his energies on the potential criminals in the world he was sure would eventually find and victimize them. Even his initial fear the divorce portended a diminished standard of living for mother and children was mostly supplanted when the little boy took proactive measures preparing his necessary defenses against all possible criminal intruders.

Later that horrible evening and after he was certain his mommy wasn't watching, the little boy, plucky and determined, retrieved from a kitchen drawer a butcher's knife which he promptly hid between his bed's box spring and the frame rail on the side of the bed next to the wall. This weapon was for his immediate personal protection. The next day, he placed under his bed a red-clay brick from the backyard and found a 2-foot-long piece of 1/2-inch rebar in the garage to augment his arsenal; very soon, a heavy glass snow globe found its way on top of the end table next to his bed, as well. He even stashed an ice pick in between two of the couch cushions in the living room.

Chapter 7

T' he hits would keep on coming the following Saturday when the children were instructed to wait outside the front of the Corbin movie theater after the matinee, where they expected their mom to pick them up. As they waited for the cream and copper Buick coupe, a shiny new 1964 Ford Thunderbird pulled up to the curb with Mom riding shotgun and a strange man in the driver's seat. Jack Norman was the man's name and he was Mom's new boyfriend. Jack was a rocket scientist from N.A.S.A. in Houston and temporarily assigned to work at Rocketdyne as a mission specialist for the Gemini space program. To say the presence of another man so soon in Mom's life was a shock to the little boy would be an accurate statement; however, it wouldn't be too long before dismay would become a better descriptor.

Jack Norman, let's face it head-on, turned out to be an asshole. The little boy knew nothing of the phenomenon but Jack had it all in spades; he carried a little rat-bastard Napoleonic complex during his every waking moment, a pompous man in all things. Just to look at his handwriting that was so stylish and exacting revealed a self-righteous perfectionism the little boy feared correctly would later bring him into disharmony with this four-eyed runt.

The one positive trait the man held, unlike his dad who really didn't care much for sports, Jack was a total jock; this meant the little boy would be encouraged to *play* baseball, not just *watch* the game. Yet, even this had a downside since Jack never met an athletic activity he didn't love; and since the little boy thought games like football and basketball were stupid sports to begin with, there was some early friction until the child recognized the more virtuous path being his compliant cooperation with Mom's new friend. For a while... at least.

The little boy contracted measles in early September and missed the first week of his 4th grade in school. It would be his last year at Tarzana Elementary and the last year of residing in the Collins Street house. Because the school semester started out on the wrong foot, the little boy, now a week behind everyone else was totally lost within the class curriculum.

His teacher, a Mr. Grogan, was a very disagreeable man who communicated in a manner the little boy found hard to interpret; going so far one day to argue with him a contrary point that, regardless *that* the word "ketchup" was spelled as it was, he insisted the word when spoken was not pronounced phonetically and was indeed pronounced as "catsup" irrespective of its spelling. With the onset of divorce, the little boy had begun a new level of contempt for authority and although this jaboney was the first and probably most deserving teacher he ever really hated, Grogan wouldn't be the last authority figure the little boy would find despicable.

A mixture of fear and contempt, along with equal measures of respect and an odd adulation for "authority" will be a lifelong source of his basic dysfunction; the little boy would simultaneously feel contempt for it at the same moment he sought its approval. The stems of this peculiar form of neurosis are rooted in the dilemma developed earlier wherein he feared for his safety when his dad was present and feared for his safety when his dad was absent.

For his 10th birthday, his mom treated the little boy to the most wonderful surprise. For once he received a gift that was something he truly wanted; a Schwinn Stingray bicycle. Now, it wasn't exactly outfitted as was his wish, but it was the real deal and it certainly was close enough... it would be called "awesome" by some kid today, to the little boy, it was "boss" when Mom was within earshot and "bitchen", everywhere else. Although the divorce would not be final for 7 more months, the family was irrevocably splintered and knowing it beyond all doubt, the little boy had stopped referring to either parent with two syllables; it was now and forever, just Mom and just Dad.

He was minding his business on the day when one of the neighbor kids let the little boy know that something was up with his mom way down the block and out of sight of home. It was reported that she just happened to be parked elsewhere in the neighborhood with what appeared to be a new bicycle on the roof of a Volkswagen Beetle, Jack Norman's real car. (The T-Bird of months earlier was only a temporary rental.)

Apparently, his mom admonished the other child not to spill the beans, but that didn't stop the little boy; curious to see what was up, he denied knowing anything and claimed to be just randomly happening by on his crummy old Huffy. When his mom saw him she immediately got pissed and shooed him away before he got too close and thereby avoided having her own disappointment in the surprise being spoiled. He didn't mind that she got mad, he was way too happy to be a little boy with a new bike sporting that fat "slick" tire and the banana seat that made the bike so popular. This little kid was residing in a new kind of heaven, but pretended for just a moment he didn't notice the lime-green wonder-ride. He would now ride in style on a bike just like his friend Nick Stewart rode.

She probably had to pinch and scratch to be able to afford the cost of the bike on her own, but she made sure there was no doubt that the gift came from her only. Under the circumstances, there was no way at this time his dad contributed to the purchase; however, it was quite possible some of the money was borrowed from Jack Norman. Certainly, she borrowed his car, which had a roof rack, to bring the bike home from the shop and since the cost of a Stingray bicycle was around $50 in 1964 (about $365 in today's dollar), it's reasonable to assume her boyfriend helped his mom out with the purchase. Nevertheless, and to sharpen the point made here, she and she alone, gave the little boy that gift.

One day while on a neighborhood excursion, each riding their Stingray bicycles, his friend Nick Stewart and the little boy made a typical stop up the street at Jake's Jug for a candy bar. While riding back toward home, north on Wilbur and as Nick was in the lead and just crossing where Philliprimm Street intersected their route, a car traveling northbound passed the little boy and turned right onto Philliprimm Street.

The driver, a middle-aged woman who claimed she never saw Nick before making her turn, collected the child and his bicycle and crushed both between her car and the curb at the very apex of the corner. Of course, she stopped immediately once she realized she had hit *something*, which minimized the injuries to Nick; but his bike was totally destroyed. The little boy saw everything happening right before his eyes and before the carnage concluded the horror convinced him with certainty he surely would find Nick pinned underneath the car, dead as squashed. Fortunately for a tough little kid, Nick stayed out from underneath the car's wheels, only suffering a broken wrist and a busted pair of eyeglasses.

After completing the first semester of 4th grade, there was a change of teachers and the little boy, no longer an antagonist to the wretched Grogan, would see better grades and have an easier, more productive time learning. The new semester also brought a refreshing surprise in the name of an adorable girl, new to the school and named Donna Dash; now his classmate.

Although Donna liked his friend Ricky Russell more than she liked the little boy, she was a fickle little cutie and easily played one boy against the other. She and the little boy would run races at recess between the dodge ball court and a building where the water fountain was located, then back. Somehow, he instinctively knew he should let her win every once in a while. Sometimes Ricky and the little boy would hang out at Donna's house that was a big two-story Tudor lookin' thing, built on a huge lot with a swimming pool around back.

Donna, was not exactly a rich kid, she was the daughter of parents just moving into a more upscale neighborhood, her father being a Hollywood film technician previously living in Van Nuys Van Nuys. She could have been from Mars for all he cared since the little boy was absolutely carried away by her infectious adorability. He would feel inside him a warmth for that little girl he immediately mistook for love, which before he knew it would be nothing but a sorry memory of the past. Unfortunately, recollection would skew into something less than desirable and would be the source of tremendous inner conflict as the little boy grew into manhood.

A mature observer would recognize as predictable the tactics employed in the earlier skirmishes between the soon to be warring divorcées. The only card his dad held was total repentance, which manifest in the unspoken but nevertheless very clear promise that he would never again lay a hand in anger on the little boy. His mom, on the other hand, was nowhere nearly as restricted by way of the propaganda with which she would fill his and sister E.D.'s ears. Although subtle at first, after time the vitriol flowed easily as it filtered through the children, whom became mired in the middle through the processing of vile swill hurled between the two adults.

In late May of 1964, the adults came to an initial divorce settlement that included full custody of both children awarded to their mom and their dad was allowed one (1) four-hour period per week for visitation privileges. During the children's summer break from school, their dad would be allowed full temporary custody for an entire week and was allowed to take them anywhere as long as their mom agreed to the destination in advance. Dad was also ordered to pay Mom $70 per month in child support.

Although Dad's visits were not supervised, he was nevertheless compelled to keep the children within his immediate care and to never leave the physical boundaries of the San

Fernando Valley. To that end, their dad should have been waiting for them at the Tarzana home every Wednesday afternoon and returned them by 7:00 o'clock that evening. For the time being, this was to be the sole extent of his contact with either child. In fact, and despite the court order, the little boy's dad never once arranged to visit him or sister E.D. for the remainder of their time at the Collins Street home and no explanations were ever offered, either.

As the school year came to an end and summer began, the little boy would enjoy the beginning of his time off with a case of contagious impetigo. It started on his right knee as a small, red sore that soon began leaking (in words later made popular by John Lennon) a yellow-matter custard dripping from a wound that defied healing and tenaciously continued to spread its own gooey issue to other parts of the same knee, then his right elbow, and eventually the left knee and left elbow, too. At its worst, the wound to the right knee was a pus-oozing open sore spread about 2 inches in diameter across his kneecap. The little boy was beginning to think he had leprosy, but the adults never became alarmed enough to do anything to alleviate the condition. "Here, spray the damn thing with this Bactine" and, "oh, hey, here's a Band-aide."

Jack Norman had a camping trip planned in which he would treat the family for a full week and would take them first to Yosemite for two days, then a drive through the Sequoia National Park one day and a trip to Devil's Postpile Monument on the way to Mammoth Lakes and Hot Creek another day. The big finish would be a day in Bishop, California for the annual "Mule Days" celebration. They would sleep in a tent, cook by Coleman stove and roast weenies and marshmallows on a campfire. Jack Norman taught the little boy how to pitch the big tent they would all share, also how to use a hatchet to split firewood and how to light the stove, lanterns and campfire. Although rather cramped driving for hours in his Volkswagen Beetle, a grand time was had by all... until they got to Hot Creek.

Things didn't really turn ugly, but they did get a little scary;

and, for the little boy a run-in with an invisible geyser caused him
a fair measure of pain. The topography at Hot Creek has changed
as time changes most things. In 1964 there was a tributary of cold
water that ran into a big fissure in the earth at which bottom was a
natural geyser perpetually boiling the water pooling into the gaping
hole in the earth. The water lingered for a while in the basin being
heated and mineralized before spilling out into an eastbound
distributary of a rapidly rushing stream about forty feet wide and
of varying depths up to six feet or so.

Casting himself about the edge of the great water basin about
50 feet away from where the main geyser was bubbling up in the
virtual center of the main body of water; the little boy found what
looked to be natural egress into the water, which looked
deceptively benign. It was a shallow ledge, similar to a swim step
built into many swimming pools, only a foot deep and beckoning
him to step there to comfortably enter the hot springs. What he did
was to wade headlong into a seemingly innocuous and shallow
pool containing harmless looking, yet treacherously hot and not
quite boiling water.

After stepping where he shouldn't have, the searing pain to
his feet and legs caused him to lurch out of the water toward shore
where he collided with both knees and elbows upon hard, not-so-
motherly earth. The impact skinned up both his elbows bloody,
opened the barely scabbing pus-filled lesion on the right knee and
spilled fresh blood from a new tear on the left knee; and all of it
would in two days transform into a new and rapidly spreading
yellow contagion he would soon learn was called impetigo.

The scary part of the day came later that afternoon when the
little boy and sister E.D. ventured into the creek downstream from
the geyser that gave the place its name. Unfortunately, the current
soon overcame them both and may have perhaps swept them both
to their death had they not been excellent swimmers. Regardless
the outcome, they were each quite frightened at the time and each
knew with some odd degree of relief there was not another soul
around to share in the experience and/or help them from a

potentially inescapable situation. After extracting themselves from the grip by which the stream held them, they briefly enjoyed a slightly closer bond than they usually held on other days past.

After returning from the week in the wilderness, reinjured at the hot springs and literally oozing away, the adults decided the little boy probably needed the immediate care of a medical professional. The remedy of choice in 1964 for this impetigo was a large dose of penicillin; administered by injection on two consecutive days. Curiously, the first injection elicited no adverse reaction, nor did the second injection; well, not at first. Indeed, there was no reaction visible until the following morning when the little boy awoke and first saw himself in the bathroom mirror.

This summer would be the first time his mom trusted the little boy to mind himself without a babysitter and to also look out for sister E.D., as the sole person responsible for her day care and well-being. By the time he woke that morning his mom had already left for work and apparently didn't notice the little boy's condition. When went to take a pee and looked at himself in the mirror, he saw a vision of a boy he couldn't recognize. His head seemed to him to be nearly double normal size and was covered in red welts or "hives"; all the other portions of his flesh that were not raised into red and blotchy welts were pulled piano string tight and were pure white in color. The little boy's whole body was afflicted just as horribly as was his head.

Quite alarmed, the little boy immediately called his mom at work and told her of his condition. Having tried to fool her in the past by attempting to skip school through one feigned malady or another, his mom was well aware of his capacity for hyperbole when it came to complaints of illness. Except... school was out for the summer vacation, so why would he exaggerate about something like this? Perhaps motivated by the outrageousness of his description of condition, his mom returned immediately home to care for the little boy.

Once she arrived and assessed the situation it became

evident to her that immediate departure for the hospital would be most prudent. He would spend the next 7 days at the Northridge Hospital; in a double room he gloriously didn't have to share with anyone else until his last two days of admission. With the daily afternoon broadcast on Channel 9 of the "The Million Dollar Movie," the little boy would watch the Elvis Presley feature film "Loving You" every single day of his stay in the hospital, and twice each on Saturday and Sunday. Suffice to say, that particular movie is permanently etched into his memory, as are all the lyrics to all the songs and will be to his dying day.

Before August of 1964 came to an end, the children would learn of their mom's decision to move the family into a three-bedroom apartment at the corner of Parthenia Street and Tampa Avenue, in Northridge; a little more than four miles north of the family's old Tarzana home. This news would not sit well with the little boy, not at all. Even though there were plenty of children living at their new complex and he would have access to a heated swimming pool anytime he wanted, there was something much more precious to the little boy he would lose and these new circumstances were scant consolation to assuage his anger at an opportunity for love now slipping from his reach.

As if grasping for something to make it stop, he made perhaps the worst mistake of his life, he confided his innermost feelings to his little sister, E.D.

Ever since the scary incident at Hot Creek when they were both swept uncontrollably downstream a fair distance and of course, his collision between medical necessity and the unfortunate limitations inherent in the science of antibiotic pharmacology, the little boy had invigorated in himself a better appreciation for his little sister and of late had vowed to demonstrate a greater degree of respect for their kinship.

So, he shared with her his most intimate secret and told her not to tell their mom what it was. He was in love with young Donna Dash and in being forced to leave Tarzana was horribly crushed he would never see her again and he would never have that special feeling for another person, ever, ever again. Now, it might have been a mistake, almost as if a dare, to ask her not to tell their mother, but who can really know why she did what she did; she might have flapped her jaw no matter any admonition, or none at all. Nevertheless, blab to Mom is precisely what she did and she did so at her earliest opportunity. The fucking little bitch.

Regrettably his mom's reaction was not entirely unexpected, but sister E.D. ratting him out was indeed a big surprise. Rather than sympathizing with him and reply with: "Don't worry honey, there will be plenty of pretty girls for you to meet and fall in love with during your time here on earth", that someone might expect a normal mother to express to her 10-year-old son in the middle of a messy divorce and a dysfunctional home life; instead, he was forced to suffer a teasing he mistook for abject ridicule.

However, like every other goddamn thing that turned to shit, the fault would be ultimately his. Yep. Why the fuck would she want to show the little boy any compassion; after all, wasn't he, the little bastard, *really* the person responsible for *her* divorce? Furthermore, his mom's cavalier expression of attitude seemingly granted license to sister E.D. to chime right in as well, parroting the ridicule hurled his way from Mom.

The taunt was akin to something only a child would do. Irrespective that her own immaturity might excuse the inappropriateness of this response to her son's very real and truly intimate feelings; nevertheless, she filleted them with scant regard for how he might interpret such scorn and derision.

"Donna Dash, Donna Dash, Donna Dash; guess who's got a girlfriend, guess who's got a girlfriend? You've got a girlfriend, you've got a girlfriend; who's the new girlfriend, who is she, who is she; she's Donna Dash, Donna Dash, Donna Dash..." and repeat... constantly. As if it was a BAD thing that he should have had these feelings for another human being in the first place. Regardless of the motivation of either female to mercilessly tease the little boy about this secret, neither cared a wit that the boy's sense of loss was real. The girl wasn't even close to being a "girlfriend" at all and these two bitches decided to pick at his scabs rather than offer their sympathy and support, much as he sympathized with Mom and tried to support her after she lost her husband. They simply didn't give a shit at all about the fragility of his feelings.

None of the little boy's sensitivities were ever considered at any of the dozens of other instances when either his sister E.D., or their mom, or both in unison would repeat the Donna Dash mantra above. The only thing he took away from this one stupid moment of candor was that this little boy's need for a girlfriend was the epitome of weakness and *that* would NOT be tolerated, by either of the two females with whom he lived and would be stuck with for some time to come.

Certainly, this is an unreasonable response to a little friendly teasing, right? Nevertheless, that is what happened and the little boy was so embarrassed by this Donna Dash business he stayed as far away from girls as possible the whole remainder of his childhood, into young adulthood until he moved entirely away from the family home. For the record, the last time sister E.D. uttered the taunt was when he was 14 years old, while his mom stopped doing it about a year after the razzing began; but by then it was too late, his fate was already sealed.

If they were ever going to tease, taunt and ridicule his very existence ever again, he sure as fuck wasn't gonna give them anymore fuckin' ammo. The resentment harbored over this matter ran very, very deep. Moreover, there were valuable opportunities lost in which to otherwise learn the proper way to treat girls and women in particular; as well as the rest of humanity generally. The price he paid for missing out entirely on all levels of such crucial interpersonal education is incalculable. "Who's your girlfriend? The unattainable Donna Dash, that's fucking who, idiot." The taunts seemed to him inescapable.

Unrecognizable to a nine- and ten-year-old for its advancing decrepitude, the apartment building, indeed the entire neighborhood, between the east/west boundaries of Tampa Avenue and the Aliso Canyon "wash" and the north/south boundaries between Parthenia and Napa Streets, consists of block apartment buildings that, in 1964-65 were on the verge of becoming a gang-infested barrio nearly 100% Latino occupied. The white exodus from this neighborhood was still five or six years away, by which time the family would be long gone. Today, this 60 or so acres are among the most dangerous in the San Fernando Valley west of Reseda Boulevard; with every square inch of it under 24-hour videotaped scrutiny of all the gangbanger's neighborly activities.

What was otherwise clear to the little boy was the undeniable fact the family's wherewithal was effectively cut in half and the real fear they would advance in poverty instead of retreating from it was never lost on him. Indeed, and even though the sorry future condition of the neighborhood was not yet in evidence, the vibe of living there filled him with a palpable, ever-present dread; a part of which was certainly influenced by this dismal new locality alone.

The unsettling decision of his mom's new course correction barely sunk in before the school year began at Napa Street Elementary; and in a flash, he began his 5th grade. From the moment the divorce was announced the children had scant contact with their dad in spite of a court order requiring weekly, limited visitation. It wasn't a matter that his visits were denied or obstructed by their mom; instead, he was having difficulty arranging his work schedule to accommodate his new lifestyle. Which was certainly as good an excuse as any, but little consolation to the little boy living without a dad.

Even in a matter as pedestrian as the visitation order, the two adults would again foist surprise upon their children; for neither child was aware, on that first Wednesday after the semester began, that their dad would be waiting for them when they returned home from school that day. However, there he was, waiting for them and seated on the stairway leading up to their second-floor apartment located in the northeast corner of the building. Before they began the climb upward, he jumped up and descended to meet them at ground level whereupon he escorted them to his Monza parked at the curb in front of their apartment building.

"Come on kids, were going to get you some reindeer." It's true that the little boy and sister E.D. had begun to grow apart in recent weeks given her response to the Donna Dash revelation; nevertheless, he always joined her in the walk home from school every day. Other than that, with the days of Smokey the safety boy protecting her from errant shards of glass now being long gone, she was left to be and play with her own friends and he would go mostly his own way without her tagging along.

Regardless of their gradual isolation from each other, the excitement they both experienced on their way over to the May Company at the Panorama City Mall had them tittering and scheming about what name they should give their new pet. This was a really special event; hell, Christmas was still three months away and they were going to get a big jump at it with this day's present and all the other kids living in their building would be really jealous.

Once they got to the big department store and saw there was nothing immediately apparent that something as exotic as livestock was being sold - hell, the store didn't even offer goldfish - all too quickly was the fire of an unreasonable desire quenched when words spoken earlier, which the children entirely misinterpreted, were more clearly expressed.

It seems the real reason for the trip to the mall was a follow-up to their mom's efforts three weeks earlier when she brought them both to the very same place for new clothing for the new school year to come. Their lives, post-divorce would now be controlled by court order and the agreement of the parties to comply with that order. So, it was agreed their mom would spring for the clothing and their dad would pay for and assist in the acquisition of "rain gear"; and eventually new shoes and overcoat and/or jacket, if necessary.

It wasn't going to be a furry new friend, as they both believed they would be getting, but rather, a new rubber suit for each of them. "Rain *G*ear?" Not, rein**deer?** What the FUCK?

The disappointment of learning the truth was bad enough; but, in the little boy's case, his dad's demand for adequate weather protection included no alternatives respecting style. There was only one choice available this day for the little boy, a tremendously dorky costume made out of bright yellow rubber coated canvas. A pair of rubbery, baggy trousers with elastic suspenders that was large enough to slip on over his Levi's; together with a jacket of similar material and a silly hood permanently attached with a bill which made him look like a human bird-boy attired in something a 5-year-old shouldn't ever be caught dead wearing in the age of the Beatles and the Rolling Stones.

His sister E.D. would be spared similar embarrassment simply because there were alternatives to little girl's "rain gear" that didn't look stupid at all on a schoolgirl and she was given a choice. Sister E.D.'s choice was a clear plastic, knee-length coat with pretty little flowers silk-screened all over. Shit, the little boy would have had a better time of it wearing her get-up than the official uniform of the Napa Street nerd brigade; he now being their only friggin' member. The little boy's choice was determined for him.

His trouble with the other boy in that first semester of his 5th grade began with ridicule and continued when he revealed his weakness and its associated hot button for the others to press at will, and it all began with that fuckin' rubber ducky suit he was forced to wear to school on days whenever rain threatened to drool over the Valley. Oh, let's not forget his very snazzy haircut wherein his very fine hair was sculpted to make the top of his head flat as a tabletop, however, necessarily forced skyward by combing dollops of Butch Wax through the stubble. Foolhardy foibles foist upon one fucked-over fan of the Fab Four.

Once the sport of pushing his buttons became apparent to his other classmates, there seemed an endless stream of participants eager to get in on the fun. That is, until two boys took matters a little too far one day and the others were finally able to rein in their own merriment. Of course, it was the violence these particular two brought to the picnic that ultimately dissuaded the others from continuing; although none of those who withdrew ever saw fit to alert the teacher of the little boy's plight, which grieved him most of that semester.

It was a gradual thing. First, the wound would be revealed, and then they began to pry at it with their words. Regrettably, the little boy reacted and let them all know they were picking at a very sore lesion. He was being forced to wear this yellow obscenity and that compulsion to him was clear confirmation of *all* the abuse his father foisted on him and here it was for everybody to see in the bright light of ultra-nerd. He simply couldn't deny the truth this was an entirely stupid outfit since he was the only kid in his grade wearing such an ugly and childish abomination. He could easily... well, maybe not so easily... handle the abuse suffering in silence and under cover of a private life; but what he could not bear was to let others around him know he was actually living a dysfunctional life, 24/7. The way the little boy saw matters; this miserable new outfit was an unfortunate extension into public view of an embarrassing private existence.

There inevitably came time when the original troublemaker and his best pal began to believe their taunts amounted to "fighting words" and inquired of the little boy his reason for not defending himself as was expected of someone whose manhood was so sorely challenged. Then something so bizarre happened to him there is no explanation for it, except for how it taught him to behave once he had an opportunity to start fresh at another school. For the time being, he would take the beatings... plural... and did NOTHING to fight back, ever. It was not a matter of a personal fear of getting beaten, he could easily suffer through that well enough; indeed, his true fear was rooted in how badly might another person be injured if he should strike that person in anger. He simply didn't want that responsibility. That is not to say he was complicit in this process; he just wasn't certain how to break the chain of abuse they hurled at him once it began.

After the first semester of 5th grade rolled into the second semester, the joy of terrorizing the little boy just sort of wore off. Some of the players were placed for one reason or another in other classrooms and things for him settled down into normalcy with a minimum of conflict. The little boy and sister E.D. kept their weekly visits with their dad and they all began to look forward to summertime when he promised the kids another delectable surprise during their week-long, court ordered, summer "vacation" in his full-time custody.

"Goody-goody; what could it be? What are we going to do?" they each wondered aloud and to themselves in anticipation.

"You'll just have to wait and see," he said.

When spring of 1965 arrived in Northridge the little boy enrolled in the local Little League Baseball organization, where their playing field was located on the edge of the railroad tracks running almost parallel and 200 yards to the north of Parthenia Street, very near the Wilbur Avenue intersection. Although his mom made it possible for him to sign up for the League and arranged for him all the particulars, there was more than just a nudge of help from Jack Norman in the process. Jack too, signed up at the same time to be the assistant coach of the same team on which the little boy would play. The man was taking on an even greater role in the growth of the family and despite his evident Napoleonic intensity; both children were encouraging their mom to marry the guy, if only for the sake of *her* happiness.

One evening Jack Norman accompanied, even as his guardian, the little boy to a "father/son" event held after supper when all the boys his age at school were invited to a frank "sex talk" in the school's auditorium. It was mostly a technical discussion about the ins and outs of reproduction without a single description of anything remotely in-'n-out related. All chemistry and no mechanics are the best description of the exhibition. If he were willing to accept as possible his mom would allow the defiling of her body in the manner rumor would have him believe, he may have inferred the correct mechanics from the chemistry illustrated. However, since his mom had so far proved so extremely uptight about human bodily functions, he was certain he could hear her ass squeaking when she walked, which offered him proof positive that fucking was something his mom would never, ever do.

Even afterward he was more confused than ever; except, during an uncomfortable Q&A later at home, the one or two questions burning his subconscious was wondering if any of this stuff had anything to do with Mom's soiled undies hung up all around the bathroom once a month and those nasty gobs of wrapped tissues tossed in the bathroom's waste basket. Although the big picture was painted for him and these technical issues were explained, there was still an enormous gap (no pun: were talkin' about someone's mother here, sicko) between these details and the assumption the adults made that he was *willing* to do the necessary "arithmetic." Maybe if they'd have given him the equation: $P+V=B$, he may have solved for "B" much earlier. Nevertheless, the fact was the little boy never heard or saw anything at that slideshow demonstration that specifically addressed how dick met and entered pussy and he left the exhibition that evening essentially uninformed.

Although still a horny little sprat; however, as to actual knowledge of the crux of the matter... he was entirely clueless. "My Mom! I don't care what you say; she would never do something like that. Not ever!" he afterward exclaimed to his school chums.

However, this specific objection was not at this moment voiced and nothing graphic was really even so much as vaguely implied, if even that much; so, the message they were trying to impart was incomplete and would remain so until the summer after his 6th grade ended. Jack Norman did his part... sort of, but it was a time when few people were as mesmerized about sexuality as are people today, so the presentation and later discussion was not sufficiently informative in this instance.

With the onset of Little League season came sad revelation that the little boy couldn't hit the ball a lick; okay, he was actually a pretty good fielder, but he finished off that first season with an .060 batting average. He got his one and only hit, out of seventeen total at bats, during his first time at the plate when he, eyes closed tight, took a Hail Mary swing at a pitch that got in the way of the bat and he made his one and only visit to first base the whole season.

His team at Northridge Little League was the Cubs and when the standings were finally tallied, the Cubs were league champions, in spite of the little boy's presence among them. Except that he would be otherwise occupied vacationing with his dad and sister E.D. when the awards were presented, he would nevertheless receive a trophy for the team's efforts; of which he was quite proud to display thereafter in his bedroom for years to come.

Adrift on a sea of parental foolishness and essentially friendless, the other adults in his life seemed all too eager to add to his misery. Take that first year playing Little League baseball for example: Although it was abundantly clear he was deathly afraid of being hit by a pitch while standing at bat at home plate, the team's assistant coach, one Jack Norman, encouraged management that the best way to cure the little boy's fear was to make him a catcher!

So, the little boy went from being a ball player who couldn't hit to a totally ineffective catcher who now literally pissed in his pants while squatting behind a chunk of wood swinging above his head and trying to catch a ball hurled directly at him with eyes completely shuttered. No part of this experience was helpful on any level, but that didn't matter; Jack Norman was a catcher; and a quarterback; and a scratch golfer; and a track star and by God, the little boy was going to be an athlete if he was ever going to be this man's stepson. So, the fuckers in charge started with catcher.

All the while, his immature (for a 10-year-old) behavior did nothing to help him advance any meaningful friendships. When he did find some measure of camaraderie among his fellows, such as on the Little League team, something awful would happen to drive others away from him. Regularly pissing in his baseball uniform more than once was one such example and there were many others. Sometimes his own actions would bring him difficulty and other times his parent's involvement in matters would cause him sufficient turmoil and embarrassment he regularly patterned his behavior into one of cowardly withdrawal. Suffice to say that by the time the family left Northridge and moved to Sherman Oaks just before the summer of 1965 ended, the little boy would have no one in his life he could safely call a true friend.

His isolation was pervasive and imposed itself on his fragile psyche with very odd effect. Whenever trouble found him and ordinary life became less so under the pressure of some conflict giving him pause for inner reflection, such moments were always accompanied by the self-inquiry of... "Before I became me, I was minding my own business and had zero problems. Now that I am I and me at the same time, nothing ever happens that doesn't cause me some measure of pain or humiliation; exactly, what the fuck did I do to cause me to be born into this nest of certifiable lunatics?"

The phenomenon adjoining the question was always a succinct and crystal-clear inner awareness that the individualized nature of his conscious self (although quite separable from the physical self at any particular moment in time absent God's grace), such self-same consciousness can never be separated from its own identity... EVER, not even under death shall the two ever part.

Moreover, there would be no escaping the fact it was he, and he alone who was the individual solely attached to this particular conscious awareness of which only he possessed. It would be true in this lifetime and it would be true in the next lifetime, as well. Wishing it weren't so; nevertheless, he knew he was the one who was fucked and knew it would be he for the duration.

If there was one thing he would take away from his childhood that he felt he could always bet the ranch on, it was this most basic truth. Unfortunately, without an adult's guidance, these very adult thoughts only managed to further isolate the little boy and left him with no one in which he felt he could confide.

No sooner did the ink at the bottom of the application for divorce dry than each parent began to implement their own brand of hyperbole to drive a wedge between the children and the other parent. Mom had a distinct advantage insofar as the kids spent much more time within her sphere of influence than they spent with their dad. Each of them employed a different approach and the misinformation hurled at either child was very subtle from the start, yet as time passed and the kids remained un-persuaded to adopt their dad's way of thinking, the effort for their allegiance intensified to a degree most uncomfortable.

The argument employed by each at first was simple: from their mom they were encouraged to remember the awful past and Dad's violent outbursts of anger; from their dad they were encouraged to consider how unfair it was *to them* that they didn't have more time to spend with him so he could continue 24/7 being the new kind of dad he was becoming. Of course, he demonstrated his sincerity in all this by continuing to bestow upon them goodies and trinkets at each of his weekly visits. While Dad was taking a page out of his parent's playbook respecting his kids and shamelessly attempting to buy their love, Mom was trying to scare their love for him plum out of them. Two sick fucks masquerading as adults, with grave responsibility to mold into society two civilized individuals and whom, each threatened by the other, were to escalate the combat by throwing the children into a cauldron of needless turmoil and putting responsibility for it all smack on *their* shoulders.

Enter the bimbo.

The divorce would be final in May 1965 and the children would be spending the last week of June with their dad; staying alone with him for seven full days without the buffer their mom would otherwise provide. Indeed, this would be the first time *ever* their dad would be allowed alone with these children for much more than just a few hours at a stretch. *In their entire lives.*

They would be spending the week at "Uncle Allen's" cabin at Lake Berryessa in Northern California. Uncle Allen was related to Gramma Beryl somehow, yet his capacity as uncle was entirely nebulous; although everybody called him Uncle and dad claimed himself to be his "nephew", the man was in no way a literal brother of Gramma Beryl's. Whatever, whomever... so far, all the evidence gathered revealed Gramma Beryl's relatives were all possessed of a very tenuous connection to the old lady herself. Beyond that, every one of the folks on her side of the family were oddly reminiscent of a species known to drag their knuckles when they walk.

So, it came to the day their summ... the very *fucking* day... their summer vacation with dad was to begin... both children would receive the shock of their lives. He told them earlier there would be a big surprise coming this day and he was NOT exaggerating.

Waiting for him at the curb with bags packed, Dad showed up at the apartment at 8 o'clock that June morning driving a strange car with a strange woman sitting shotgun beside him of whom the children had NO idea would be a feature anywhere near their expectation of this coming week's reverie. Moreover, the appearance so soon and without warning of a new person anywhere near the manifestation of a *stepmother*, who would now also remain a permanent fixture in their lives, struck the little boy immediately as rank and utter betrayal. Nevertheless, a new stepmother was exactly what Jean now was to both the little boy and his sister E.D.

This transfer of custody from Mom to Dad would be the first

time either child would be spending any meaningful time with Dad since the day he showed the little boy how to shoot his service revolver over a year earlier; and now there would be a complete stranger to accompany them that would effectively alter their preconceptions of the entire trip on one hand and the rest of their lives on the other. WHAT THE FUCK? Not even their gutless mom had the courtesy of giving fair warning of what was to come and it simply wasn't fuckin' fair for these adults to treat their children with this level of disrespect. There was absolutely no way this turn of events came as any surprise to their mom on the day of their departure; regardless, she played a dummy just as baffled as the kids.

Jean was a school teacher who would (many years later) be revealed as Dad's girlfriend going all the way back to the little boy's awful run-in with a glass door. She was the teacher's assistant and they'd had a fling-thing going on all these years, a mistress totally on the sly one minute and a faux mom the next. By the time of their official union under law Jean was a Junior High School teacher teaching 8th grade "Social Studies" to kids three and four years older than her new stepchildren.

Apparently, she assessed her new kid's maturity level and found it lacking; therefore, much of the next six hours were occupied by the children learning about such diverse things as homosexuality; that some people became drunk from smoking something out of a "pot"; and scariest of all, the existence of a motorcycle gang calling themselves the Hell's Angels and the threat the family faced from theses criminal hooligans simply by venturing north during *this* very trip.

The kids were only 9 and 10 and going on the first real vacation with just their dad and this bitch felt compelled to feed them this kind of shit all the way to their destination. At least there was no talk of the issue of custody on the drive-up Route 99, nor for the first few days of the vacation; however, on the return trip there would be talk of little else.

Chapter 8

*L*ake Berryessa was a magical place in 1965 and one could easily imagine living lakeside for a lifetime, being completely content with nothing more than a small powerboat, some water skis and a good fishing rig and tackle. Uncle Allen's "cabin" was situated within the confines of the Spanish Flat Resort located about 2 miles north of the southwest tip of the lake on the west side of 165 miles of shoreline. The lake, 26 miles long and about 3 miles wide, is the largest manmade lake in California and just a stone's throw east of the vineyards of Napa; California's highly vaunted "wine country".

After six hours and weary from relentless traveling, the children were finally notified their destination would soon be nigh. Most of the last ten miles of the trip seemed to him an eternity of swaying back and forth over winding roads characterized by gloomy shadows in which sunlight, obscured by countless roadside oak trees, was prevented from illuminating the route anytime other than high noon. Upon reaching the lake's main and southernmost distributary, the road began to straighten a bit while the lake and the enormity of their new playground came into full, panoramic view. From the car's vantage point, the wonderment of first sight replaced the disorder of the journey and the little boy was instantly captivated.

The sign greeting the family informed they were entering "Al's Sugar Shack" and their new stepmother was beside herself with outrage, apparently more focused on Uncle Allen's blatant expression of cocksmanship than the dilapidated condition of their new home for the coming week. The little boy didn't really understand what the woman was harping about since all he could see was nothing more than a "crazy little shack" cobbled onto and integrated within a 16' Airstream "Clipper" trailer that hadn't been roadworthy in a decade but was now perched on concrete blocks 100 yards from water's edge. What Uncle Allen lacked in accommodations was entirely rectified in the boat he made available to the family for the week. It was a 28' Chris Craft day cruiser and perhaps the finest watercraft coming out of the Spanish Flat cove at the time.

The kids would learn how to waterski and fish and barbecue and that it was okay to pee in the lake. They would play 25-cents per game 8-ball pool up the hill at the modest general store in the evening and wake at the crack of dawn to the sound of boating fisherman and early morning water skiers tearing up the lake before breakfast. The little boy would quickly learn that lake conditions were ideal at dawn and soon would be out there with the other early birds while the lake was still smooth as glass.

Both children would master skiing on two waterskies very early that week and by the time he would be offered his last ride on skis for the summer, the little boy would succeed in conquering the slalom ski and would be ready to master it the next time they visited Lake Berryessa. This is the point where, again, the shit would hit the fan with such tumult that his mom's relationship with Jack Norman would begin to derail and the little boy's distrust of her would be cemented into an ever-expanding wall of irreversible emotional isolation.

The adults with temporary custody of the kids were quite patient in establishing the set-up; waiting, waiting, waiting until the children expressed the notion of the return trip, they began to expect would be possible for the next summer in their dad's custody. This was the time when the adults made their move and suggested that the kids wouldn't necessarily have to wait until next summer; why, they might just be invited to return in nearby September, if they played their cards right.

The hook was set, now to land the fish would require the adults to choreograph a delicate dance of coercion and convince the children the key to returning in two months' time would turn in the lock solely on their ability to convince Mom it was their idea and their idea alone to return for a second vacation that summer with Dad and Jean.

Once the cat was out of the bag, the adults put on the full-court press to convince the children it was best if the news to Mom came directly from their mouths and not the adults with conflicted interests. Before this occasion neither child was fully aware of the bitter seriousness, nor all the underlying ins and outs of the custodial battle between their parents; especially now that another party's interests were also entering the mix. Suddenly and without realizing they were stepping directly into the fire of bitter custodial passions, the children willingly offered themselves up as the inflexible instrument of a perverse tug of war for their *affection*... of all friggin' things. These "grown-ups" were some sick, twisted individuals.

Hell, making the decision to appease their dad and new stepmom was easy; to agree to the suggestion was indeed the immediate and simplest course of least resistance. However, the kids were soon foiled when the adults made it clear the ball was entirely in their court to, not only make good on their promise, but also to stand up against their mom in defense of a desire (they were not aware they had) to spend more time with their dad. This was where he knew full well it was going to get very dicey, so the little boy put the whole matter out of his mind for the rest of the week. In this particular round of tempestuous Yahtzee, the little boy had rolled 5 snake eyes. Winner, winner... but no chicken dinner.

Meanwhile, they each had a blast learning to drive the boat and getting more comfortable on water skis. Between the two kids they must have caught 300 bluegill fish sitting on the bow of the boat anchored in one of dozens of out of the way coves in abundance around the perimeter of the lake. The fish were never bigger than about 4" long and were useless for anything but

entertainment so the kids dutifully tossed every one of them back
to be caught another day.

Early in the week they found a spot in an isolated cove where
a huge tree along the shoreline failed to grow perpendicularly and
with branches strategically overhanging water that somebody
already discovered was the ideal position to anchor a tremendous
rope-swing for all and sundry to enjoy in turn. The take-off point
was a bluff carved out of an eroded shoreline about eight feet
above the waterline.

On the Friday nearing the end of the week they decided on an
excursion to the rope-swing one final time this trip. When they
arrived at the cove where the attraction was located, there were
about two dozen teenagers already congregating and essentially
monopolizing the rope-swing, so the family stayed back for a
while just to marvel at the youngster's boisterous antics.

Eventually, a boy about 16 or 17 years old took up an
extreme position from which to launch himself into the water that
resulted in an awkward separation of boy from rope and a wild,
coincidental reaction wherein that rope whipped upward toward its
anchoring point high up the tree's trunk and became snagged in the
overhanging branches; leaving the rowdy teenagers with the object
of their immediate merriment completely inoperative.

The teenagers were obviously lake regulars; indeed, the cove
was very secluded and they all necessarily had to arrive by boat of
which four beautiful ski boats were tied to various tree stumps on
the shore nearby. The pretty young girls all had titties blossoming
under bikini tops and the boys, exuding testosterone all around,
now began to hammer on the culprit responsible for cutting short
their day's amusement.

Although the thought didn't immediately occur to the little
boy, it was just as probable as not that one of these boys installed
that rope swing onto the tree in the first place. Nevertheless, once it
was apparent the older boy would have to climb up that tree,

retrieve the rope and man up to his own responsibility for what had occurred, the little boy became very fearful there would be a terrible accident. He was certain if the boy fell from the tree at that height, where the water directly below wasn't more than a foot or two deep and strewn with large rocks just underneath the surface, they would all see him die right on the spot.

The little boy was horrified at the specter before him. Not the fact alone he might see a person die this day; it had more to do with how his own future would unfold and what it means to have to take responsibility for one's actions out in the real world. Basically, he began projecting all the unknown ways in which he may be personally tested, as the coming unknown particulars of his life were slated to eventually transpire. The incident revealed to him several subtle, yet unsettling implications about the responsibilities expected of adults and what would soon be expected of him, too.

The thing of most significance was an epiphany of sorts in the certain knowledge that, if necessary, he too would climb that tree if ever he were cornered in similar circumstance. He wouldn't like it, but he knew if push came to shove, he would take his medicine, climb that tree and free the rope. Or, so he thought.

In witnessing this random demonstration of a group dynamic, an example of human interaction far different than anything in his previous schoolyard experience, the little boy was astonished how these teenagers reacted even *after* the matter was efficiently and successfully resolved. Of course, had he looked backward and recalled the time he saved the children of the Lazy J Ranch certain death by fuzzy black spider, perhaps his expectations would have been more in line with the groupthink of the teenagers present and the behavior they exhibited toward the object of their ire.

Even after the older boy's victorious accomplishment in restoring the operation of the rope-swing and putting his own life on the line for some stupid childish laughs, instead of being greeted with a hero's welcome after setting foot on solid, though muddy earth, the humanity comprising this group had no intention of rewarding that boy for fixing a fuck-up the mob deemed should never have occurred in the first place. Rather than offering any acknowledgement of gratitude, the other kids instead continued to hector the boy until they eventually became occupied by some other distraction.

By now, both the little boy and sister E.D. were committed to the notion they would be returning to Lake Berryessa with Dad and stepmom Jean this coming September. Unable to speak for his sister's level of commitment, he was certainly aware of the clock ticking against the ominous responsibility *he* now faced; to which role his own level of commitment was definitely, but secretly, beginning to waver. Since they wouldn't be returning to Northridge until Monday late afternoon and the fact he was powerless in locating a wormhole by which to escape his fate; until then, he sure as shit had no other choice but to put the whole pending magilla straight the fuck out of his mind. Pronto tonto.

As they pulled the Chris Craft away from the cove that afternoon, the impression left from the visit to the rope-swing was indelible and the little boy was awash with confusion and helpless recognition he was fucked three days hence and with nothing he could do now to prevent **somebody** from being hurt. Neither could he and sister E.D. avoid getting stuck with having to pay the freight for the selfishness of four manipulative adults.

The intrepid water rats would have just three hours the following morning to get in some waterskiing and as dawn cracked, the four of 'em were very first on the water. Since he had much improved, the little boy got first crack at opportunity and managed a deep-water start and generous turn to ride a slalom ski on water flat as a sheet of glass. The feat allowed him to proudly leave the lake that morning a bona fide, intermediate level water skier.

By noon Saturday they were all packed up and ready to begin the final phase of their weeks' vacation with Dad; a trip to the San

Francisco Bay area, a drive over the Bay Bridge and the Golden Gate, then through the city and down Lombard Street, a cable car ride and capped with dinner on Fisherman's Wharf. Saturday afternoon occupied most of the driving part and nighttime found them taking up temporary housing at another of Dad's relatives of nebulous lineage; an Aunt Wilma and Uncle Milton living in nearby Walnut Creek. Why were none of the relatives they met ever related to their dad's Dad? Strange.

Aunt Wilma was a childless homemaker, while Uncle Milton was a deaf painting contractor and a big-game hunter of some national renown. Their house was even more upscale than was his dad's Dad and Gramma Beryl's house and was predominately decorated throughout with frilly, old-lady type things interspersed with dozens of wild animal "trophies".

The little boy was at first quite excited to learn he'd be bunking in the den, all alone for the night on a hide-a-bed with an enormous stuffed Caribou head fastened to the wall directly above him. Later in the dark, with nothing but strange shadows slicing through the distant streetlight outside and casting themselves upon the many lifeless former organisms present, he suddenly became less thrilled with his new "uncle's" avocation and the idea of sharing a room with these pointless sacrifices.

Of course, being himself a gun nut, he would never begrudge Milton his hobby. It just seemed to the little boy an arrogantly selfish exercise to take a life if only for the rank gratification of having something to occupy empty wall space; what with no suggestion Aunt Wilma had any Elk meat handy to feed the kids.

It was during this leg of the trip that the adults did a strange thing. They began in earnest to treat the children as if they too were now little adults; this behavior expressed itself in a manner neither child had ever before experienced.

Particularly so when dining Sunday evening at Alioto's Restaurant on Fisherman's Wharf, where they were joined, not only by Wilma and Milton, the little boy was surprised to find Dad's dad and Gramma Beryl would be joining them for dinner, as well. Of course, this must have been a relief for Dad since dinner here with all these people was going to cost a lot of money, of which "Grampa" would now be obliged to cover and which his son would shamelessly allow. As events transpired, the opportunity to behave like little adults extended late into the evening and served well to postpone the inevitable. While nursing his Shirley Temple cocktail the little boy was given temporary reprieve from wondering exactly how the fuck was he going to find the balls to confront his longsuffering mommy the following evening.

The drive home Monday morning started out with the presence of considerable stress given the task ahead and the fact that the adults occupied themselves hounding the children with promises of more benefits available to them if only they took the opportunity to spend more time in their dad's custody. When it became clearly evident they were nearing their destination, the little boy's apprehension began to overwhelm his ability to think clearly and he was consumed with absolute dread in the knowledge he was going to now have to eat his own cooking. At the same time, he felt oddly betrayed by the manner in which the responsibility for any of it should fall on his and sister E.D.'s shoulders. He knew they both were essentially tricked into saying yes to Dad and Jean, whom were now going to make the kids each *really* act the adult, just like they were acting in the restaurant the night before.

Although he understood essentially nothing about contract law and even less about the nature and scope of the conflict between his parents, sitting in the car that long drive home, the little boy was so consumed by the specter of the pending encounter with his mom that, had his thinking not been diverted by the fear, he may have actually recognized in himself the fool for which he was now being played by Dad and stepmother Jean. With cynical behavior initially entrapping the little boy and his sister E.D. into a scheme to circumvent the court sanctioned divorce agreement and knowing well in advance their mother would never acquiesce to the trick, these two pieces of shit went ahead anyway and determined to exercise against two helpless children a morality of dubious inspiration.

Despite the certainty of his epiphany at the rope-swing cove three days earlier, when the passion of conflicted desires began creating perceptible friction, instead of shouldering the burden, the little boy melted like a chocolate bar basking in the sun. Rather than own up to his personal responsibility in making the nefarious decision, the little boy cowardly lobbied and cajoled and coerced his little sister E.D. all during the ride home to take the lead when time came to delivering the bad news to their mom. Somehow it worked and she agreed to be the first one to speak on the subject when they arrived.

Of course, Dad and Jean made it clear that this was not something that could wait; they would not be satisfied unless the matter was entirely settled that afternoon so they could go about making plans for September unencumbered by doubt. The adults made it further clear they would accompany the children into their home upon arrival and they would all have a discussion like grown-ups to iron out the details of a forgone conclusion. Except... their mom still held veto power and nothing about this adult conversation would be foregone; including the wrath of a mom pissed.

When Dad and Jean returned to their own home that evening (and the children remained with Mom and the also present Jack Norman) and despite their expectations, which began the day affirmatively planning for the September trip, the newlyweds nevertheless departed with assurances less certain than a definite maybe. However productive the negotiations may have appeared to Dad and Jean, and irrespective of inferences falsely indicating a mind open to possibility, the only person who mattered, having already firmly committed to another outcome, didn't mind stringing them along until she could straighten out her misguided children.

At the heart of this entire matter was the written court decree and Mom's demand for that precise document to be the only fucking order by which they were ALL going to abide and they weren't making any stinking changes, goddammit. Who can blame her? She paid good money for that document, as she was the declarant petitioning for the original terms of divorce. It was the law and she would hold the cop and the schoolteacher to the very specific intent of every single word.

Unfortunately, at this so-called meeting of adults, Mom and Jack Norman didn't express matters to the children in quite the same language they would soon adopt to impress upon them the intractability of Mom's presumption of strict loyalty expected of her children. Certainly, they weren't going to show their cards to the other players during negotiations.

Apparently, they came to believe they couldn't just put their "foot" down and tell it like it was... Nope. Instead, this pair of brave adults would also put the weight of decision back upon the kid's shoulders, occupied now with so much guilt there was no longer enough space for them to even think cognitively, much less rationally. Nevertheless, it was going to be their decision to make and Mom and Jack Norman were going to help them to understand exactly how to make that decision *correctly*. This process was to begin that evening in just an hour or two; they would have supper first, and then their own meeting of "grown-ups" would ensue to discuss the business at hand and how to resolve their differences.

Coincidentally, the management of their apartment building was throwing a 4th of July party that evening for all the tenants and select guests. There was going to be a rock band and food, drinks and great fun was slated for all, except two certain children just arriving from a week's vacation at Lake Berryessa. Those sorry people and their crazy guardians were all going to enjoy a white-knuckled drive around the greater Los Angeles area in the Volkswagen Beetle their mom now used for transportation; having by this time traded in the gas-guzzling Buick for her own economical "Bug", just like her boyfriend drove.

Jack Norman got behind the wheel, Mom rode shotgun and the kids sat on the bench seat in the back. Trapped in the car and being mercilessly scolded, the little boy as usual and for the next three hours experienced his usual shrinking phenomenon until it felt like his head was just resting without a neck on the Naugahyde covered padding as they bounced aimlessly down the road.

Their route was a familiar one traveling south on Tampa Avenue to Victory Boulevard, then west to Topanga Canyon Boulevard, south some more and up the grade into the Santa Monica Mountains, past the little community of Topanga until finally reaching the Pacific Coast Highway. From there, Jack Norman turned the car south again and they continued driving down the Coast Highway its entire length until reaching the City of Long Beach.

Upon reaching Long Beach and the night time sky was as dark as it was going to get, the little Bug joined up with the 405 Freeway where Jack Norman, satisfied the point had been sufficiently driven deep into the exhausted children, finally turned north and headed for home some 45 miles away. Remember, those same kids had earlier that day endured a 6 hour, 400 hundred, some-odd mile drive home, while continually fretting over the possibility this very torture they were now suffering would result once they expressed the simple and not too unreasonable desire to spend a week with their dad just to have a little summertime fun.

Regrettably, neither the little boy nor sister E.D. possessed an adult's comprehension of the threat their mom perceived to her custody "rights" and the coming onslaught from the newlyweds challenging that custody. Neither did they comprehend the motivation of the bride to secure for herself ready-made children for *her* own family; which just so happened to be bereft of sufficient sperm cells to fertilize her child-craving womb. This particular dynamic was completely lost on the little boy; however, there can be little doubt his mom was well aware of the underlying implication of her ex-husband's impulsive vasectomy years earlier.

Although none of these intricacies spilled out during this ride of tears, the haranguing that began simultaneous with the turning of the Bug's ignition switch was the most bizarre case of two "adults" intimidating a 9- and 10-year-old into hating their dad's new life and fearing any further breach of their mom's sensibilities.

Once uttered, it was obvious to the children their "wish" to return to the lake in September was a regrettable decision and one in which they must immediately reconsider. Blessed was the fact the hectoring was so steeped in irrationality that memory of the incident quickly faded into the kind of black hole a drunk has at his disposal to wash away the previous night's depravity. With but one exception, there is no way now to recall the entire dialog spewed their direction. Nevertheless, what is known is that their mom and Jack Norman took turns employing a myriad of tactics to impress upon the children the whole measure of their displeasure of the fact the kids had acted independently to upset the specifics of the official divorce decree.

In search of a rationale compelling the children's pliability to reason, the adults in turn issued a rambling diatribe intended to humiliate, embarrass and intimidate. Suddenly, the dialog got really bizarre and this occurred early enough during the hell-ride that faint memory still wanders the ether, when Jack Norman asked the little boy a most confusing question apparently intended to gauge his level of commitment. He began delivering his baffling harangue just as they were cresting the highpoint on Topanga Canyon Boulevard, a place on the map known as the "Top 'o Topanga" and where the road immediately begins to meander downhill all the way to the coast, as did the common sense of these two goofy adults.

Once in the car, the kids were immediately pummeled with bitter words expressing a certain level of sour disappointment Mom had in her children; whom were by now well apprised of their mistake, were attempting to backtrack from their position and disavow any desire to return to the lake that summer; not for a week, a day, or even an hour! Except, their reversal was not good enough or fast enough for that other psycho now in their lives... the odious Jack Norman.

Apparently, Jack wasn't too keen on reading the signals of their complete capitulation and feared the subject would resurrect due to a lack of commitment within the heart of the little boy. From that premise he exclaimed, "If I gave you 50 dollars, would you agree to never see or meet with your father ever again?"

Not having a clue as to why he should be motivated to ask such an incongruous question, the little boy became completely lost in what seemed like an episode of "The Twilight Zone".

"If that's what you want me to do, I guess I'll do it."

"Yes, but will you take the 50 dollars?"

"If you want me to stop seeing my daddy, I'll stop seeing him and you don't have to pay me anything."

None of this line of questioning made a lick of sense to the little boy, but too bad; Jack Norman just kept at him, "If your father gave you 50 dollars, would you agree to stop seeing your mother?"

"Look, I'll do whatever it takes to get you to get you off my fucking back," was the little boy's unspoken plea. In the first place, the sum of $50 was a complete abstraction to a 10-year-old in 1965; that amount of money then was a large sum for a child. Hell, it was an amount of money his mom probably didn't even have in a savings account at the time. Even if he possessed anywhere near that amount of money, he would have no clue (beside saving) what he would do with it, so the question held no significance to him as the money offered was essentially meaningless and the base proposition an entirely absurd notion.

Furthermore, just how the fuck did money have any connection whatsoever with any part of this conversation? Was

Jack Norman saying there was an equivalency between a monetary value and the natural desire of a child to have a little fun with his dad for one measly week at the end of summer? It was a sick and very immature line of interrogation that succeeded only in confusing the little boy and ultimately creating in the man to be a cynical vessel quite capable of regurgitating vitriol into an imaginary void the moment it entered his vague awareness.

For a little boy humiliated and a propensity to shrink emotionally, if not in actual physicality, and who heard clearly the message intended the instant it was delivered, there seemed no point for either of the adults to continue the verbal pummeling. In anger not easily assuaged, they just continued harping at and belittling the kids until they fell silent in their own exhaustion.

Needless to say... there would be no trip to Lake Berryessa in September. Furthermore, two weeks wouldn't pass before their mom received a summons demanding her return to divorce court to renegotiate the terms of the settlement in general and the expanded sharing of child custody between mother and father, in particular.

The new bride was staking her claim and the children were reduced to malleable objects ripe for exploitation. Ever in the middle, the terms revolved around their portability on the one hand, and the only leverage their mom possessed on the other hand; i.e., their father's ability to pay Mom the toll (child support) in exchange for time (theirs). The kids, the children of these *"selfless"* adults, were nothing more than a commodity available for barter and swap; and a degenerate system of family justice lets people get away with this kind of crap every day.

She pulled the kids out of school that day, dressed them both in their best courtroom appropriate finery and they all trotted off to the City of San Fernando, at the north-most portion of its namesake Valley, to face justice head on. She had coached them each thoroughly on the off chance they might be called to testify; a precaution uselessly taken since at this time there was never going to be a situation in which she would lose primary custody. Perhaps that was indeed the endgame, however that prospect did not present itself even in the moving papers presently before the court.

Another thing never in doubt was the fact that their dad was going to be awarded more visitation privileges with the children. Now that he had a partner in his new wife, someone the court recognized would relieve the burden of his work schedule vis-à-vis custodial visits, the court was inclined to give him something pretty close to what he was asking for.

Ultimately Dad was awarded one entire weekend, once per month and one full Sunday, once per month; as well as granted full-time custody coinciding with his summer vacation with the L.A.P.D. and expanding the duration of that time to three consecutive weeks per year. For these concessions, the child support payments to their mom were increased nearly 100%, to a total of $135 per month.

To a little boy lost amid parental irrationality, the court decree was nothing less than alms for flesh. Or maybe, it was arms for hostages? The truth all depends upon one's vantage and perspective.

Chapter 9

*B*efore Mother remarried in 1968 the family would move into two more residences, at the end of summer 1965 to Sherman Oaks for two years and then to Canoga Park until July 1968.

Perhaps the relocation was responsible or maybe it was just confidence exuding from personal advancements made that summer at the lake, the newfound ability to drive a boat, the skill to operate, if not yet master a slalom waterski and the savvy to shoot a game of 8-ball pool. Regardless of origin of motivation, once he began to interact with the new kids at his new Sherman Oaks school and his fellow 6th graders, the boy carried about himself an ever-present shield; a combination of distance and distrust melded with an attitude soon reflecting an underlying force-field of subtle intimidation.

Although a fact, it is doubtful that any of the other kids were ever indeed aware he vowed to pummel any or all of them into pulp if ever challenged as he was in the 5th grade. Although the tactic worked flawlessly and he never again faced a physical confrontation at the hands of his classmates; nevertheless, behavior of this nature would exact from him a steep price in the end.

The wall he erected around himself served him well on one hand and on the other was his greatest obstacle. Especially when measured against his inability to experience any meaningful social interaction without running away when conflict arose and while the only two arrows in his quiver were the noise of a bully and the menacing intimidation of a lout.

The boy, once a man, never meant anything personal by any of it; for he was essentially a shithead to everyone within his sphere no matter how much he thought he cared for this person or the other. God forbid he thought poorly of anyone; if so, they were toast in his eyes and usually discarded without much ceremony.

Indeed, his determined behavior was not motivated by personalities per sé, and was completely defensive in nature, even if random observation seemed to witness a contrarian viewpoint. Had his methodology met with any measure of resistance, there may have been more choices made evident to him under other circumstances; however, having met none, he behaved according to his inner vow to allow his classmates to abuse him never, ever again. To say his manner was passive-aggressive is bald understatement.

Kester Avenue Elementary School was a 3-minute walk north while Van Nuys Junior High was a 10-minutes to the east, then a 3-minute walk to the north. The Little League field was another 5 minutes farther east of the "middle" school. It was a good thing all were close by too, since the boy had his precious Stingray bicycle stolen right off their patio soon after moving into the apartment and he would have to walk everywhere until earning enough money babysitting, or pulling weeds, or doing other chores for the manager of the apartment building, to be able to afford to buy another bike. He was a fairly ambitious kid in that way and always very proud of setting goals like that and achieving them.

The boy did well enough in math and science and excelled in English, history and shop class. He held his own with algebra and biology but was stumped by geometry and chemistry. He got along well enough with the other kids, was generally cordial, helpful and kind; however, his ability in making friends was always difficult or strained. Although he didn't ask to continue with Little League, Mother insisted he participate until he was no longer eligible after turning 12 years old.

Mother's relationship with Jack Norman terminated shortly

after the family moved into the Sherman Oaks apartment and the boy was grateful for its expedited closure. Although the incident didn't drive the last nail into the coffin of their relationship, there can be no doubt she questioned his wisdom when Jack Norman resorted to employing a suffocation technique in his first and only attempt at administering corporal discipline unto the boy.

The altercation between Jack Norman and the boy occurred in the swimming pool at the Northridge apartment, late summer of 1965. They had gotten into a fracas over Jack's perception the boy (standing in the shallow end of the pool) did something untoward against sister E.D., when he forcefully splashed water in her face responding to one of the countless irritations she would employ in her endless effort to get his attention. Standing on the deck, high and dry and being suddenly and intensely incensed, Jack Norman immediately retaliated on her behalf by jumping from the deck and landing right on top of the boy, whereupon Jack commenced to holding the boy's head underwater until getting slugged in the side of his own head by the youngster.

Needless to say, to the boy, this attack was the ultimate affront and entirely reminiscent of the spark that destroyed his satiny Roy Rogers cowboy suit three years earlier. But, because he swung a fist in anger at Jack Norman, he was certain a beating wouldn't be too far behind so he bolted from the pool, the building and the neighborhood wearing nothing but a pair of black Rayon swimming trunks. No shoes and no shirt, he wandered around a while until finally taking refuge in the dugout at his Little League field for an hour or two until finally being discovered by his mom canvassing for him in her navy-blue VW.

Relieved to see her all alone and offering no resistance, he ventured over to the car expecting a mother's gracious absolution; given that he was convinced there was by no means by which he should be considered the aggressor. His mom didn't exactly see things his way and was as pissed off as she could be. Upon returning to the apartment and with Jack Norman having long departed for his own home, the boy was sent to his room, this being afternoon at about 4:30, where he stayed the remainder of the day and into the night... of course, without supper. Although deprived of food this night only, he was to stay in the apartment every day until the following Saturday and was not permitted to venture outside the whole time.

Although ruffled feathers were subsequently reorganized between the boy and Jack Norman, there was another factor entering the picture that hastened the ultimate and permanent separation. Jack Norman's assignment from NASA, Houston to Rocketdyne, Canoga Park had come to its natural conclusion and he was preparing to return to his own home. Although willing to uproot the family and bring them with on his return to Texas, he wasn't prepared to adorn Mom's hand with either a wedding band or an engagement ring. Jack Norman was gone before Christmas 1965 and would never return.

Although he would eventually discover most of his weaknesses, the boy never let any physical limitations hamper his enthusiasm for waterskiing, Little League and various other activities that attracted him. Like most boys, he probably imagined himself much better at those things than he actually was in practice.

For example, playing baseball he was always an excellent fielder, but he couldn't hit for shit. It wasn't until the second to the very last time he would be eligible to swing a bat in Little League that he would hit his first and only home run. In fact, it was an inside the park, 2-run homer that would ultimately win the game and clinch the division championship for the season. He was proud about that one for as long as the immediacy of the memory lasted. As for his waterskiing ability, the boy really believed he was cutting a mean groove in that water, in reality he never became any better skilled than a mediocre intermediate skier, no matter how many jumps and cutbacks accomplished, by which he dazzled mostly just himself.

Regardless his form or lack thereof and stilted perception of his actual level of skill or ability, he did his best to be the best and made no apologies for less than stellar results.

The boy learned in Junior High that he was destined to be a natural-born metalworker and took to metal shop like he'd been working with the stuff his entire life. By the time he turned fourteen he had already learned to weld with an oxy-acetylene torch and he could electric-arc weld like a pro before leaving high school. Ultimately it would be the boy's metal working ability that gave other boys his age pause to consider him a worthy human to include among them. Well, that was the boy's perception of things, anyway.

Once the boy's ability became evident to the metal shop teacher, who would by way of example for the others in class, bring attention to the work the boy had done, he began to enjoy a measure of respect theretofore apparently undeserved and otherwise unremarkable. Okay... he was beginning to get it... it didn't matter what it was a person pursued, what mattered was that they pursued something other people could not do; or better yet, learn to do something others were *afraid* of doing. The boy, in this case, became very skilled at metalworking and did indeed slip from obscurity into a member of the student body and ultimately into society, even if only as a grimy jack of trades.

Despite the newly renegotiated divorce agreement with the terms of custody more favorable to Father, at no time during the next three years was the issue of child custody ever too far away from the boy's day-by-day existence; indeed, any recollection of the subject matter overwhelms all other memory of the times.

Although Mother was just as guilty as Father for conducting custodial warfare using the children as swords one minute and shields the next, she did not pay an immediate price for the behavior as far as the boy was concerned. The same cannot be said for sister E.D.; who, once a teenager, held a lifelong resentment against Mother, although not so much against Father. There was a constant effort by Mother to poison both children with reminiscences of Father's past; while Father seemingly left it to stepmother Jean to play mind games with the boy's (and sister E.D.'s, too) already well-established Catholic guilt in attempt to sway (their) loyalty in Father's direction.

Father never again struck the boy once the divorce was announced and he departed the family home; indeed, there was only one time in the next five years that he even had occasion to exhibit any displeasure at all with the boy and even then, Father kept his cool. While yes, his demeanor toward the boy post-divorce never reached a level of threat similar to the past, the fact Father left it to stepmother Jean to carry on the war for permanent paternal custody was never lost on the boy, by any means. Whether Father was aware of the exact psychology she employed was not really important to the boy since he presumed at minimum, Father tacitly approved of her reprobate device. Naturally, as these events built one upon another, the outcome resulted in the application of an equal measure of resentment against his father and stepmother alike for their rogue efforts to divide him from his mother.

The children were slated to visit Father and Jean on Christmas day of 1965 at their rented 3-bedroom home in West Los Angeles. They picked up the children the afternoon beforehand to spend some time at Father's father and Gramma Beryl's home for Christmas Eve, where they exchanged gifts with the Grams after having dinner at a nearby four-star restaurant where "Grampa", as usual, picked up the check. Afterward, they would drive to West L.A., spend the night and wake to the now discredited Santa Claus, the opening of presents and the usual Christmas morning cheer. Although "Santa" was so very generous to the residents of that house that morning, the children returned to their home and Mother later that afternoon completely empty handed.

Not only was Mother incredulous and outraged, the children each felt quite cheated, as well. After all, wasn't it their own mother herself who made considerable effort to ensure both her children embarked upon their Christmas visit properly bearing gift offerings, not only for Father *and* his parents, but *also for their new stepmother* Jean, too. Even though the kids wrapped the presents themselves, those gifts were the product of their *mother's* time, effort and expense.

After the preliminaries, the hot cocoa and the cinnamon buns in snuggly bathrobes and the oohs and aahs uttered upon gazing at all the stuff found under the tree, they got down to the business of opening presents........

"Wait, wait... before we do that, let's go out to the backyard and see if we can find the reindeer tracks," decides Father, speciously invoking Christmas myth.

So, the four of them, girding for the winter chill, all schlep out the front door, around the side of the house and its tall wooden fence to the backyard gate, of which Father, with exaggerated ceremony, swung open to reveal... a 16' Tahiti semi-V bottom ski boat with a 100 horsepower Johnson outboard motor, sitting on a trailer and a set of Taperflex water skis perched on its seats.

After more oohs and aahs, high hopes and big talk, the merriment resumed within the warmth of the domicile where the children were assigned to open two presents with their names written on each and found under the Christmas tree. There were two identically large boxes and they tore at them voraciously; only to find each box with the same thing inside - a water skier's floatation belt, each personalized in black calligraphy. Father and Jean then opened their presents, which the children brought for *their* Christmas while all the rest of the presents under the tree remained there unopened for the balance of the day.

Since there wasn't a lake nearby their Sherman Oaks home and they didn't have a suitable car to get to it even if there were, there was no cause for the children to believe they would be taking **home** the boat, motor and trailer... the water skis... was there? Not even their own floatation belts, with their names scribbled on each, were sent home with the children that Christmas. Mother was pissed on so many levels and for good reason, too; these fucks were now resorting to offering bribes similar to what the asshole Jack Norman had offered the boy just six months earlier. Regardless the outrage expressed, Mother's indignation wasn't necessary to convince the boy that Father and stepmother Jean were shooting very dirty pool here.

Apparently, Father was never fully aware of the tentative nature of the trust he was being afforded by the boy during these years. Since there had been no inkling violence was still an option, everything had been very harmonious and all parties made the best of circumstances. However, incidences like this Christmas present business were wearing thin on a boy with sharp wits and the facility to take care of himself without as much reliance upon help from his elders. When the final indignity permanently displaced the boy's trust so much that severance was inevitable, it was indeed the action of the wicked stepmother Jean cementing his resolve.

The kids would visit Lake Berryessa three more times; for 3-weeks each of three consecutive summers, in June-July 1966, 1967 and 1968; always concluding each trip on July 6 or 7. By the summer immediately following the very first of their trips to the lake, Father and Jean bought and substantially improved their own trailer and attached cabin that was palatial compared to Uncle Allen's rustic hovel nearby. Father's new lakeside villa was his and Jean's free and clear and sitting on a graded parcel in which they held a 99-year lease on a prime chunk of Spanish Flat real estate.

During each of the three subsequent trips, both children would expand their boating, waterskiing and pocket billiards skills and for the visit that would amount to the last summer they were subjected to the custody agreement, they were even allowed to invite and bring along a best friend apiece; E.D. brought Cheryl and the boy brought Johnny. The children always had nothing but a great time at the lake and when it was all over and the lake would no longer be there for him to enjoy ever again, the boy would discover those trips to Lake Berryessa and the Spanish Flat resort to be fond memories sorely missed.

Mother met her new husband Kevin at a "30 and over" singles club in Encino called the Ventura. Widowed, with a 16-year-old daughter who had her own horse and was being pretty well spoiled since her mom committed suicide a year or two earlier, Kevin was a city surveyor and did pretty well for himself under his pay grade. Mother and he hit it off from the beginning, as did the boy and sister E.D., each of whom begged Mother and prayed to God they should marry. Plans were laid for the purchase of a 5-bedroom house in tony Granada Hills and the wedding slated for mid-July 1968... after completing the scheduled three-weeks' vacation at the lake with Father and stepmother Jean. It was decided the boy would spend the week Mother and Kevin were honeymooning with Uncle Frankie's family, while sister E.D. would stay the week with Aunt Caro's family.

For the preceding two and a half years there was relative tranquility and a delicate truce respecting the acrimonious child custody issues of the past with all parties surrendering to the regimen of the status quo. Let's just say status wrung quo's neck when stepmother *Jean* got word of the announced honeymoon arrangements and began a zealous effort to correct an obvious insult to her and the boy's father.

Irrespective of the honeymoon issue, the pending marriage itself was bound to interfere with Father's divorce from Mother and now, more significantly, his marriage to Jean and inability to fertilize his ever-ovulating, but unsatisfied wife. Nevertheless, what happened next certainly resulted from the collision of conflicting agendas and when this bitch let out her wrath on the children in her mint-green Skylark parked behind a Ralph's one day after picking them up for the 3-day custody weekend, she revealed in herself a truly awful human being.

They children knew something was up the minute they got to the car since Jean insisted they both sit in the back seat together. She drove silently south away from their apartment building located on DeSoto Avenue in Canoga Park, bypassing their expected route onto the freeway onramp and instead turned left on

Ventura Boulevard and made a beeline for the Ralph's Supermarket on the corner of Winnetka Avenue. After pulling into the driveway, she headed for the alley that leads around to the loading docks behind the building and parked over in a remote corner of the lot.

She then began a seemingly endless tirade attempting to bully, torment and harass the children for their effrontery and although she picked them up after school at 3 o'clock, they didn't leave the Ralph's parking lot until after dusk turned to dark. As she droned on and on about the pending honeymoon and her anger at their decision, the boy, as usual, began to shrink inwardly, sinking down into the cushion of the back seat while listening passively about what a piece of shit he was for eschewing his father and stepmother and expressing a preference to spend time with other relatives, to the exclusion of *them*. It was made very clear the children's decision was the epitome of insults. Indeed… she expressed an outrage worthy of a crime much worse than mere insult and she let them both have it with blithering bitterness.

Once exhausting the first go-round of her list of grievances, she started all over again reiterating each of the horribles until finally night fell and like a bird, she just stopped chirping, started the Skylark and drove away to begin the weekend visit with their father.

Jean, Jean, Jean… let's just leave it at this: if the boy ever had any doubt he *could ever* be swayed to revert his parental allegiance, this incident sealed his resolve to never, ever let that happen. Indeed, he would never allow Jean to become anywhere near his surrogate mother and soon enough, only the law would consider her even his stepmother, because he sure as hell didn't.

Epilogue

***Borderline personality disorder**: describes a pervasive pattern of instability in relationships, self-image, identity, behavior and affects often leading to self-harm and impulsivity.*

*C*hoice. Perhaps the most significant factor in all human existence comes down to the choices we make. That we live and die by our choices is inescapable and the consequences may be either devastating or may be glorious but is usually somewhere in between. The boy at fourteen was given a choice and for better or worse, has had to live with that decision ever since.

Considering the preceding exposé, there can be no question the boy would ultimately develop a personality disorder; the only uncertainty would be in severity, and even that could not be determined until earth made a couple dozen orbits about the sun. Perhaps if more was known about his condition sooner, this boy would not have seen nearly five dozen of them before finally getting the word. And, it was not as if he didn't try; hell, he sought help over and over again but none of the professionals either knew of the condition or recognized the behavior he exhibited for what it was in fact... borderline personality disorder (BPD).

Perhaps if the choice he made at fourteen to terminate his relationship with Father had been otherwise, the infirmity would not have degenerated into borderline. Perhaps if he decided upon an alternative course his psyche may have degenerated into a disorder more egregious than mere borderline; which is rather benign compared to some of the other outcomes possible. Of course, there is no telling either way; indeed, he could have ridden his dirt bike off a cliff at sixteen and ended all the pain and uncertainty there and then. However, what may be ascertained without doubt is that his *"pervasive pattern of instability in relationships"* is the most obvious point of departure for further investigation.

Admittedly, one of the factors contributing to his relationship problems was a gremlin of his own creation. The other factor was his mother's unrelenting and jealous possessiveness in which she held her children far too close to the vest; if not locked smack in her little breast pocket.

Where he remains culpable is again, the result of choice. Once his deeply personal admission of love for the foxy Donna Dash was expressed in confidence, the subsequent and seemingly interminable teasing his mother and sister hoisted on him compelled the internal adoption of the notion, not only that his feelings toward the little girl were an expression of disloyalty against his mother, but more devastatingly, that his desire to find love away from the nest was subordinate to his mother's needs and wishes. Therefore, he foolishly chose to never put another female before his mother as long as he lived under her hearth and in her home.

This act, indeed, the choice alone sealed his fate but not for the obvious reasons. His course of action never dispelled his desire for a girlfriend, or the constant urge for sex with any of a number of his young female classmates. He just could not allow himself the feelings that came from the earlier ridicule and he was certain the same ridicule would return with a vengeance should he bring a girl from school home to meet his mother. That occasion was simply not going to happen and he would see to it with all due diligence.

In today's world, with homosexuality discussed more by

orders of magnitude than it ever was during the 1970s, perhaps his failure to bring a girl into his life would be met with another form of ridicule at home. Perhaps a well-placed "oh yeah, he likes boys, didn't ya know that?" comment at the dinner table would have been the call he needed to compel in him the correct heterosexual boyhood response to get a girlfriend... and do it yesterday! Regrettably, that occasion never happened.

Having spent much of his young life essentially friendless, he wasn't too concerned at this time about striking up a "relationship" with a girl. Given how things now stood going into his 15th year, wherein he always had trouble even making male friends, how could he harbor the delusion befriending females would be any easier for him than was the befriending of males? The choice he made to wait until leaving the family home at 18 to bring girls... er, women...into his life was not made on any spontaneous or consciously active level. He was basically content just to let nature take its course and simply presumed his mother would somehow, someday, let him know it was okay to bring a girlfriend home to meet her. That occasion never happened, either.

Curiously, neither did sister E.D. ever express much interest in any particular boyfriend while living with Mother and Kevin and only brought her first date to the home quite late in the game. Even then, it would take a special high school event she would otherwise regret not attending, namely her senior prom, to finally crack open her shell. In truth, she waited for her big brother to leave the nest before bringing any boys around the home with any degree of regularity. Was it guilt, or fear of brotherly retribution? Her motivation here would remain a mystery.

When his new stepfather Kevin came home one evening the late winter of 1969, in a foul and nasty mood and Mother wondered why, he screamed; "Because I got a call at work today from that goddamn ex-husband of yours!"

Almost immediately and as if a surreal melodrama were unfolding in the kitchen, the telephone rang and was answered by sister E.D., whom replied, "Hi, Daddy." Immediately, she passed the phone to Mother, and after she had a few words with the children's father, directed the boy to take the phone from her and told sister E.D. to pick up the phone extension in the family room.

Father explained to the children something he could not possibly have done without tremendous pressure from stepmother Jean; who by now had lost all patience and... well, to put it bluntly was seeking to cut bait. She wanted to start her own family and if her husband could not deliver unto her the children he sired earlier, nor squirt viable semen into her horrible gash, then she was going to insist they create a new family from scratch.

He continued to inform the kids that there were plans in the works to adopt two children and that was that. Now, if the older children wanted to have any part of *their* new family that would be up to them, he was not going to force the issue and he would no longer hold either of them to the custody agreement. Oh, and one more thing, this business about adopting children was already a done deal and moreover, the man bought his family a new house... in Granada Hills of all places, a mere half mile away from their own home they now shared with Mom and Kevin. "You know son, we're moving nearby to make it easier for you and E.D. to see us whenever you guys feel like doing so."

By no means was the boy prepared at the time to make such a significant, life changing decision and neither was his little sister, E.D. Indeed, it was only four months earlier when he became all of fourteen and even though he thought he knew all that needed knowing; in actuality, he barely knew shit from chocolate ice cream. Nevertheless, the adults foolishly allowed him to make the decision for himself just as they allowed sister E.D. to decide her own fate, as well. Inwardly, the boy didn't hesitate and although he announced nothing committing himself one way or another, by time the call ended, there was nothing about his mindset that would remain to him a mystery.

The moment the handset touched its cradle; the boy allowed

immediate and glorious relief to wash over him as if an astringent cleansing the grime of false loyalty that was now and forever prohibited from sticking to him by simply hanging up the telephone. The sensation was suddenly liberating and yet, the decision he adopted effectively handcuffed any possibility he would have benefited from receiving proper adult supervision guided by a satisfactory father figure. Not a domineering personality to mold him, but otherwise someone to cast a positive influence and counsel upon a boy's proper transition into manhood.

Unfortunately, when the boy made his decision that evening, he had barely even begun to get to know anything at all about his new stepfather and was not yet even aware that he would ultimately hold little real regard for Mother's new husband, nor would he ever really respect him as a "man's man". Kevin, try as he might to replace an absentee father, simply didn't have the chops to do the boy much good in this regard.

Certainly Kevin, the man, met with the boy's wholehearted approval as a satisfactory husband for his lonely mother, now five years divorced. Yes, the boy did respect the man for what he was doing for him and would continue to do as his stepfather. In providing a comfortable home for mother and kids, ensuring there was plenty of food to eat and permitting opportunity he might otherwise have missed; for all of it, the boy owes this man Kevin his very life. However, as a masculine role model, Kevin did not measure up to the boy's expectations. Moreover, if ever there was a man who knew his own limitations... it was Kevin by God, by and through his own, oft repeated admission.

Simply put, Kevin was an adherent to the school of thought that a person was much better off if they didn't set their sights too high; that a person's birth and the economic station of one's family predetermined their ability and the heights to which they should be allowed to soar.

Meanwhile, the boy was a quick study and an all-around ambitious kid, suggesting all kind of crazy things like describing ten years before the fact how great it would be to build what is equivalent to today's modern water park, or how they should start a line of hair and skin care products marketed strictly to men. To Kevin, such childish notions were either foolish or ridiculous and something that would never be possible for the boy to accomplish. His pessimism constantly rubbed at the boy and he often bristled at Kevin's inherent negativity.

To be fair to Kevin, he wasn't a sour man, negative toward people and life in that way, not at all. However, his overall demeanor was the way of the defeatist with an attitude, which the boy rebelliously rejected.

Once when the boy wanted to do a simple overhaul on his motorcycle engine, Kevin told him he'd screw it all up and made it very clear he wanted him to have a professional mechanic do the work instead. Rather than fight the man, the boy waited until he went on a hunting trip (by which time the boy had grown weary of joining him in the killing of animals for meat he didn't find appetizing).

While he was gone, the boy stripped that engine apart, put the new pieces inside, threw the old pieces in a box and waited for Kevin to return. When the old man got home and was pulling his hunting gear out of his truck parked in the driveway, the boy fired up the motorcycle and rode right past him, down the driveway out into the street, did a couple donuts in the cul-de-sac and immediately returned back into the garage. When he showed Kevin the box of used engine parts, the man had to admit his surprise at the boy's obvious mechanical ability; "How'd you learn to do that?"

His reply, "I read about it in a motorcycle magazine" was actually greeted with the unexpected expression of a father's pride. Score one for the kid.

The question of whether he should have remained loyal to his father by choosing to allow him to continue to influence his remaining adolescence, including the consequences of this pending choice, was never discussed with either his mother nor with stepfather Kevin. Sadly, a matter this important should have involved a private, father-to-son, man-to-man discussion before an immature boy was allowed to exercise this kind of responsibility. However, at 14 years old, the boy had had enough of the relentless conflict. He was far too tightly wrapped to allow *any* of the psychos in charge any more insight into his own mixed-up psyche than necessary.

Unfortunately, the significance of a conversation he had with his dad the previous summer at Lake Berryessa was completely lost upon the boy at a time of his decision, when he really could have otherwise used the ally Dad promised he would be. Although it's possible he may have forgotten the incident and didn't factor the conversation into his decision; more likely was the fact he simply didn't realize that a little boy's fate is largely the product of the choices one makes.

One evening after a day of waterskiing, the boy confronted his father in the storage pantry of their cabin at Spanish Flat wherein he told him all about the Donna Dash business and how badly it hurt and embarrassed him as a child and still did, unto that very day. In the entirety of the boy's thirteen years of life, throughout every single memory of their relationship, his father would never tell him anything more reassuring than when he told his son that such behavior would never be tolerated under his roof. Regrettably, the boy didn't see the significance of his father's promise then, nor later when it mattered most.

Ultimately, it could be argued, the boy's decision was the wrong one and was effectively an opportunity lost. Had he chosen the alternative course of action and instead nurtured his relationship with his dad, perhaps the boy would have dodged the bullet of BPD entirely. In other circumstances, maybe he would have avoided the component of the disorder that stems from an inability to foster stability in relationships. Woulda, coulda, shoulda... there are no simple or straightforward answers to be found here.

Of course, other variables obviously influenced the whole of the boy (now a man) beyond his lack of relationship skills or the frequency with which he would willingly participate in his own peculiar fandango with the women stumbling into his life.

Nevertheless, the fact remains that significant, interpersonal lessons were entirely omitted from his upbringing, which permitted a tremendous void of inexperience during a time in adolescence he should have been learning precisely how to intermingle with the opposite sex on exactly that level; as a sexual being. However, never did these things occur during the so-called formative years and being thusly handicapped, he ventured aimlessly into adulthood a total novice in the art of maintaining a successful, intimate relationship.

Reportedly, the boy at nearly 60 years of age, still lacks for much fundamental mastery of the many peculiar intimacies of life but thankfully, he still rolls a kick-ass game of Yahtzee.